Rookwood Pottery

Identification & Value Guide

- BOOKENDS
- PAPERWEIGHTS
- ANIMAL FIGURALS

Nick & Marilyn Nicholson
and
Jim Thomas

COLLECTOR BOOKS
A Division of Schroeder Publishing Co., Inc.

Front cover, clockwise from top left: Parrot on a Perch animal figural, #6842; Frog bookend, #2603; Swan Pin Tray, #1213; Trunk-Up Elephant bookends, #6124.

Back cover, clockwise from top left: Rookwood Fine Tiles paperweight, #2921; Indian Head bookend, #6158; Cat paperweight, #1883; Beagle paperweight, #6172; Parrot animal figural, #6954.

Cover design: Beth Summers
Book design: Melissa J. Reed

COLLECTOR BOOKS
P.O. Box 3009
Paducah, Kentucky 42002-3009
www.collectorbooks.com

Copyright © 2002 by Nick Nicholson, Marilyn Nicholson, and Jim Thomas

The current values in this book should be used only as a guide. They are not intended to set prices, which vary from one section of the country to another. Auction prices as well as dealer prices vary greatly and are affected by condition as well as demand. Neither the authors nor the publisher assumes responsibility for any losses that might be incurred as a result of consulting this guide.

Searching for a publisher?

We are always looking for people knowledgeable within their fields. If you feel that there is a real need for a book on your collectible subject and have a large comprehensive collection, contact Collector Books.

CONTENTS

ACKNOWLEDGMENTS

Without the aid and assistance of many collectors of Rookwood, we would not have been able to complete this book. In particular, we would like to acknowledge the following:

The staff of the Cincinnati Art Galleries has been extremely helpful. Riley Humler was gracious enough to supply us with a Foreword, and provided introductions to individuals who possessed marvelous collections of subject Rookwood pieces. Randy Sandler gave us permission to photograph items in CAG's possession. Tammy Williford let us know when unusual new shapes arrived. And Karen Singleton skillfully prepared drawings of the last nine shapes on our wish list.

These collectors allowed us to photograph parts of their collection or, in some cases, did the photography for us: Steve Belhorn, Greg Blum, Tom Fledderman, Eunice Morrow Fleming, Jim Fleming, Bob Hoffman, Jack Kircher, Jennie Kircher, Richard Miller, Sharon Nelson, and Charles and Patricia Weiner.

Dr. Art Townley kindly supplied information on his "new" Rookwood.

Mike Murphy let us use the "connect the dots" decoder published on his website.

Bob Cooper helped with computer questions when they arose.

FOREWORD

I know I am going to sound like a fossil but it can't be helped. My kids insist that I'm older than dirt and about as amusing — that's a different story. Anybody with 30 years experience buying, selling, and drooling over Rookwood will have war stories that include many "how it used to be" tales of super cheap prices — and I'm one of them. But fossil or not, a lot of water has passed under the bridge in those 30 years and a lot of things have changed.

When I began my collecting journey, production Rookwood vases could be bought for $10.00 to $15.00 just about anywhere, and you could often sell them for $20.00 to $30.00 to somebody else. Paperweights and bookends were no different. There was little interest in them, and certainly no one had bothered to catalog and identify the rare ones. Even really nice figural pieces sold for only about twice the price of a plain vase. Like everybody else, I saw many production pieces that I mostly ignored unless they were extremely inexpensive or extremely unusual. I bought a few paperweights simply because I liked the form or glaze. If you talk to someone like Jack Kircher, who began collecting 20 years before I did, you will hear even more interesting tales. One of Jack's favorites revolves around the time he found an artist signed vellum vase in a secondhand store. The vase was not priced and Jack asked the owner what he needed for the piece. The man thought long and hard and finally said, "I got to get ninety cents for it," wanting to make more than 75 cents but not wanting to push the price up to a whole dollar. Needless to say, Kircher bought the vase.

At some point all of that changed. About ten or 12 years ago people began to take an interest in what we euphemistically refer to as Rookwood "critters." With the phenomenal success of Glover and subsequent

Riley Humler

Rookwood auctions, people became increasingly aware of the scope of Rookwood's production of animals and bookends. As prices of artist signed pieces rose higher and higher, the obvious appeal and relative affordability of critters made them attractive to both new and older buyers alike. Before long, some of the rarer bookends and paperweights were selling in the low- to mid-thousands.

As to where this growing interest will take us, I can only guess. When Nick, Marilyn and Jim told me of their plans to write a book, I was delighted. (Panic set in when they asked me to write the foreword.) For one thing, I love Rookwood critters even though I don't own any anymore. They are frequently charming, generally well designed, and often graced with exceptional glazes. Compared to the fare produced by their competitors, Rookwood critters are unquestionably fine collectibles.

One of the secret pleasures of working with dealers and collectors in the Rookwood market is getting to see the unusual and the rare. In its 87-year pottery

Foreword

lifetime, Rookwood produced some amazing items and new ones seem to surface every year. It's hard to get bored with Rookwood, even with my short attention span.

This book will do two things well: it will shock you by presenting, describing and cataloging nearly the entire scope of bookends, paperweights and animal items (many being rare and unusual), and it will make collecting critters easier and more enjoyable. It may also drive you a bit mad, as there is the frustration factor associated with collecting anything. Some of the pieces in this book will not be easy to find and they might be expensive when you do find them. Don't give up. There are countless yard sales, flea markets, antique shops, and auctions, and even these rare critters do show up once in a while. You might not find that "gotta-have-it" piece this weekend but keep in mind, the search is more than half the fun and the nice people you meet along the way are a bonus.

Think of it this way. In 30 years, you, too, can tell war stories about collecting Rookwood critters to "younger" collectors. They will politely listen as you babble on about the good old days and the great bargains you found way back in 2001. Just remember, being a fossil is its own reward!

Riley Humler
Cincinnati Art Galleries

INTRODUCTION

The purpose of this book is to identify, catalog, and provide photographs of all Rookwood shapes described in the Rookwood files as bookends, paperweights, and animal figurals, as well as selected other shapes (trays, flower holders, candleholders, etc.) that utilize animal themes to promote purchase.

This book will be of most interest to collectors who already have a serious interest in bookends, paperweights, or animal figurals. It was produced specifically with their interests in mind. However, all levels of Rookwood collectors should profit by reading our book. Advanced collectors are provided a means of viewing the totality of shapes available, allowing them to more easily determine the most desirable additions to their collections. Occasional and new collectors will be assisted in determining where to go next with a fledgling collection, and what to watch out for along the way. Those who haven't yet begun collecting Rookwood bookends, paperweights, and animal figurals will perhaps be motivated to do so.

It should be obvious that if collectors profit from information in the book, pottery dealers will need to know what these collectors might wish to buy and how much they might be willing to pay. The pictures and descriptions will assist dealers in properly identifying and pricing their wares.

Specifically, the book does the following:

- Catalogs (name, shape number, size, designer) over 250 shapes, including over 300 color photos and/or drawings;
- Provides a serious analysis of rarity/availability;
- Includes a complete price guide;
- Provides a discussion of Rookwood marks the collector needs to recognize;
- Provides means of differentiating "new" vs. "old" Rookwood;
- Includes a chapter on fakes, reproductions, etc.; and
- Provides an extensive index for easy reference.

"Why," you might ask, "would anyone write a book about Rookwood bookends, paperweights, and animal figurals?" Need is the answer. Little has been written about paperweights and animal figurals, and only one article of significance has discussed bookends — a short piece simply listing available shapes in Herbert Peck's *The Second Book of Rookwood Pottery*. With the attention Rookwood is attracting at auctions, and especially with the recent escalation of interest in bookends, paperweights, and animal figurals, it seems prudent that some serious analysis of the rarity/availability/cost of these unique pottery pieces be undertaken.

It is our intention that this book be useful in

many collecting situations. For the sophisticated collector, we offer a view of the total number of shapes that can possibly be found, and provide a means to determine the most desirable of future additions. For the beginning collector or the person ready to add to a modest existing collection, we offer a means of deciding where to begin — what shapes are most readily available and most affordable. For the person who has not yet taken the plunge, who doesn't currently own any of these shapes, we offer a look at what might be attractive about these Rookwood bookends, paperweights, and animal figurals, in the hope that a whole new wave of collectors will arise.

We vividly remember the purchase of our first set

Rookwood Pottery as it appeared in the early 1900s.

of Rookwood bookends. Prior to that we had focused our collecting on artist-decorated vases. These first bookends were a rare set in a "killer" glaze. A week or so later, we showed them to a local pottery dealer and told him we might become bookend collectors. This dealer offhandedly remarked, "Well, it will be easy; there's not much interest in these because nobody is collecting anything now but vases — especially iris and painted mat glazes." How things have changed over the past several years!

Ten years ago it was relatively easy to find common sets of bookends, such as the Rook #2275 or the Elephant #2444D for under $200.00, even in mint condition with outstanding glazes. If one of the set had a glaze problem or a firing hairline, the price was halved. Common singles could be purchased for under $100.00. Common paperweights could be purchased for under $100.00, and even less common examples seldom exceeded $250.00.

Today it is very difficult, if not nearly impossible, to find a "sleeper" bookend set, one that can be purchased at a price well below the going auction value.

We have not found a really good bargain on paperweights for several years. It seems that everyone — thanks to Cincinnati's yearly Rookwood auctions, the *Antiques Roadshow*, auction periodicals, and Internet auctions — knows about Rookwood. And every seller thinks his/her pieces are worth a fortune, whether they be artist-signed or simply production examples.

In a real sense, though, any good piece of Rookwood is worth far more than its original cost, nearly 50 to 100 times or more in almost all cases. Can you find a paperweight which cost $2.50 in 1930 for less than $250.00 today? Or what about a set of Union Terminal bookends, which in 1940 cost $10.00, bringing $5,500.00 recently at auction? Still there are some relatively inexpensive examples left. There are at least ten paperweight shapes that can be purchased for under $250.00, and several sets of bookends still sell for under $400.00.

If some of these rarer sets of bookends are bringing over $3,000.00 at auction, and if certain paperweights are being purchased for over $2,000.00, it seems apparent that many people are becoming serious about collecting bookends and paperweights. There are probably 15 to 20 of the 87 sets of bookends so rarely seen that (barring a collapse of our nation's financial structure) will always bring over $2,000.00, whenever or if ever they appear at auction. At least ten of the rarest paperweights would undoubtedly realize over $1,000.00 each, were they to be offered for sale.

The high auction prices being realized for more rare and desirable bookends, paperweights, and animal figurals might cause potential collectors to shy away. However, it seems these high prices are stimulating sellers to bring stored items "out of hiding" from their china cupboards and curio cabinets – not just rare ones, but also more common shapes. Internet auctions, such as eBay and Pottery Auction, as well as larger regional and many local auctions are loaded with a variety of shapes ranging from the common to the rare. We hope this trend continues, as we fully realize everybody wants to collect things for which he or she thinks there is the possibility/probability of obtaining what is sought — of course within somewhat reasonable financial ranges.

Before we allow the reader to proceed to the bookend, paperweight, animal figural, and miscellaneous shapes sections, a few areas of amplification/ clarification are appropriate.

With regard to assigning names to bookends, paperweights, and animal figurals, we have followed a few simple guidelines. For some of the individual shapes, Rookwood provided names on the original shape cards (see Bibliography for information on how to access these cards) and these names have been retained. However, for at least half of the shapes, Rookwood does not provide a name. In the case of these unnamed shapes, for the most part we have used the name Peck provided (see *The Second Book of Rookwood Pottery*) if it has come into common usage by collectors and is not otherwise confusing. In a few instances we have provided our own simple name when either Peck has not provided one or to differentiate between shapes given the same or very similar names.

Prices of bookends, paperweights, and animal figurals listed herein are usually based on those realized for examples at auctions and private sales over the

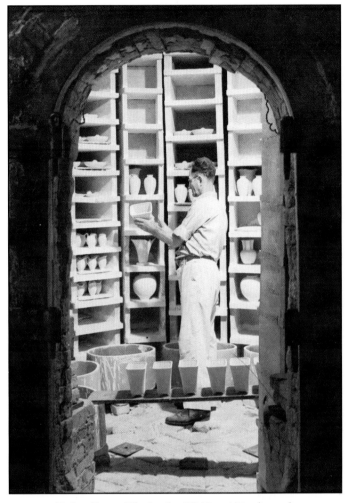

Unloading a kiln in the 1940s at Rookwood.

past several years. We always assume excellent condition for the pieces in the price guide. Some shapes have had dozens of sales and can easily be assigned a value. For these sets we list a "recent price range." Others have had only a very few sales and are, therefore, much more difficult to value; still others have failed to appear even once. In these cases, we can only guess as to the price that might be realized during a normal auction (let alone a bidding war) and have provided this guess as the "estimated auction value."

Prices for bookends are quoted for a pair (set) while prices for paperweights, animal figurals, and most miscellaneous shapes are quoted for individual items. Candleholders are generally quoted as singles, although in one or two cases, pair quotes are specified.

Unless they are rare or hard to find, 1940s high glaze bookends and paperweights are worth about one-third less than mat counterparts. Mat ivory exam-

Introduction

ples are also of less value.

With regard to the frequency with which various shapes are seen, we have designated individual shapes according to the following criteria:

Never Seen – The shape has not to our knowledge appeared for sale, and we have not been able to locate examples in existing collections.

Rare – The shape has appeared for sale only 1 – 5 times over the past several years; those examples that have appeared were highly sought after, so much so that color, glaze, and condition became very much secondary considerations.

Hard to Find – Only a few (6 – 20) examples have appeared for sale, forcing the collector to consider singles (in the case of bookends) and perhaps some amount of damage to acquire the shape.

Often Seen – More than 20 examples have appeared but there was still good competition for each; the collector has been able to apply some discretion concerning the choice of color and glaze.

Common – Examples of the shape have been found in many auctions and are frequently seen in medium-to-large malls; the interested collector has a broad choice of color and glaze.

For the convenience of the collector, we have included guides at the fronts of the first four sections. These will aid in looking up individual shapes — knowing either the name of the shape or the shape number.

In the first four sections of this compilation, we describe in detail over 250 shapes of bookends, paperweights, animal figurals, and miscellaneous shapes utilizing animal themes — candleholders, flower holders, trays of all sorts, etc. For all but a few of these we have been able to locate and photograph examples of the shape. However, in a few instances shapes are so rare as never to have been seen — even by very serious collectors. In these cases, in order to provide an image, we have turned to the original shape cards housed in the Cincinnati Historical Society Research Library. We either digitally photographed the image on the card, or

we had a line drawing of the image prepared. We thank the library staff for allowing us access to the cards.

In furniture collecting when parts that didn't begin together are made into something, that joining is called a "marriage." Experienced pottery collectors will also be familiar with the "marriage" concept from dealing with, for example, jardinieres and pedestals and pairs of candleholders. You may own a single bookend for which you find a mate in the exact same glaze color. Only if you are very fortunate will they have been made in the same year. This "set," too, then would obviously be a marriage. Married sets of bookends are worth at least one-third less than sets of the same year/glaze. This is not to imply that one should not buy single bookends — especially if the single is a rare shape or has a particularly attractive glaze/color. You may never again have an opportunity to purchase the desirable shape or glaze/color.

A word of advice to collectors would be to find a dealer, or even better, a network of dealers to help in your search for additions to your collections. It is fun to go looking from shops to antique malls to auction houses, but this will not usually net you the very rare examples. Many of our most desirable shapes have been obtained from a network of dealers, each of whom knew to contact us when rare items from our interest list appeared.

And now a final note. Beginning collectors frequently ask about the extra hole that often appears in the bases of bookends and paperweights. It is called a "fill hole" and was put there to allow additional weight to be added to these items. For some shapes, such additional weight was desirable to stabilize otherwise top heaviness. For certain bookends, the additional weight allowed more books to be supported. The fill used was normally sand, and the hole was generally closed with a relatively soft plaster after the fill was completed. We believe the auction value is unaffected by the status of the fill — empty bookends and paperweights are just as valuable as those that are filled and sealed.

BOOKENDS

Rookwood produced its first bookend shape in 1914, 34 full years after the pottery was founded. What prompted Ernest Bruce Haswell to design the Reader, #2184, or Rookwood to expand its pottery line to include bookends, is not recorded. One would assume these decisions were marketing driven – although Rookwood was not known for being overly progressive in its marketing of pottery. Bookends offered the following positives:

1. The possibility of attracting a whole new range of clients. Bookends were functional. Most potential customers of the time owned shelves of books and needed something to spruce up those shelves.

2. Bookends were potentially much cheaper to mass produce. They were molded as opposed to being thrown. Multiple copies could more easily be produced. Fewer instances of damage during firing were expected.

3. Most bookends did not require hand decoration, the most expensive part of the production of art pottery.

However the decision was made, it certainly turned out to be a good one. During the first five years (1914 to 1919), 12 different bookend shapes were introduced to the marketplace; sales were brisk, and the total Rookwood business prospered.

This compilation lists 86 numbered bookend shapes and one special bookend shape. All shapes called bookends by Rookwood on their original shape cards are included. Some of these could as well be called paperweights or animal figurals. In fact, many of the bookends would probably not be large enough or heavy enough to actually support books of any reasonable size. Nonetheless, for the purposes of this book, they are considered bookends.

We also included two shapes, the Water Lilies #2836 and the Chow Dog #6584, that are not labeled as bookends by Rookwood. These shapes resemble bookends more than figurals. Water Lilies, identified by Peck as candleholders, has a flat side similar to many other bookends, and the Chow Dog is large enough to support a reasonable stack of books.

We included the two sizes of the Trunk-Down Elephant, #2444C and #2444D, as separate bookend shapes, consistent with there being two distinct sizes of owls and rooks.

In a moment of temporary insanity we set about to estimate the cost of a complete collection, all 87 of the Rookwood bookends — if such a set could be put together. The seven common shapes could be purchased for $2,000.00 – 3,000.00. The 19 often seen shapes would cost an additional $11,000.00 – 15,000.00. The 23 hard-to-find shapes would add $22,000.00 – 28,000.00. The 32 rare shapes would cost $72,000.00 – 82,000.00, and the six never seen shapes, if they could be found, would cost $13,000.00 – 17,000.00. This brings the total collection value to somewhere between $120,000.00 and $145,000.00.

Guide to Bookends

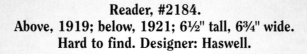

Reader, #2184.
Above, 1919; below, 1921; 6½" tall, 6¾" wide.
Hard to find. Designer: Haswell.

First appeared in 1914; original cost $20.00; most sets found date from the 1910s and 1920s; very heavily weighted set; mat blue and brown are most common colors; recent price range, $650.00 – 850.00.

Standing Colonial Woman, #2185.
1915, 5½" tall, 5½" wide.
Often seen. Designer: McDonald.

Original cost $7.00, raised to $12.00 in 1930; usually not much definition in mold; strongest mat colors (blue, green, and gold) are found in 1910s and 1920s sets; recent price range, $350.00 – 450.00.

Large Arrangement of Fruit, #2186.
1921, 5" tall, 5½" wide.
Hard to find. Designer: McDonald.

Produced in both polychrome and mat; original cost $12.00; recent price range, $600.00 – 900.00 for a mat set; polychrome will cost at least $300.00 more.

Hawthorne Rook, #2274.
Above, 1924; below left, 1945;
below right, 1920; 6" tall, 6" wide.
Often seen. Designer: McDonald.

First appeared in 1915; original cost $15.00 mat, $30.00 polychrome; by 1930 the mat set was $20.00; recent price range, $600.00 – 1,000.00; polychrome value is $300.00 – 500.00 more than mat.

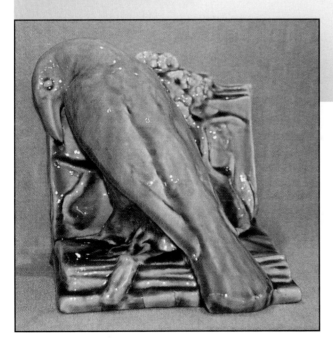

Rook, #2275.
Above, 1923; below, 1945; 5½" tall, 5" wide.
Common. Designer: McDonald.

First mold October 1915; original cost $7.00; seen both in polychrome and mat; recent price range, $350.00 – $650.00, although common 1940s high glaze sets can be found for $200.00 – 300.00.

Buddha, #2362.
Above, front and back views shown, 1918; below, 1919; 7½" tall, 5" wide.
Hard to find. Designer: McDonald.

Also called "Chinese God" bookends in original Rookwood files; first appeared in 1916; seen both in polychrome and mat; most sets will have good mold detail; original cost $10.00 mat; recent price range, $900.00 – 1,500.00.

Bookends

**Trunk-Down Elephant, #2444C.
1923, 6" tall, 7" wide.
Often seen. Designer: McDonald.**

Original cost $15.00; recent price range, $750.00 – 1,000.00, although mat ivory and 1940s high glaze sets have sold for $400.00 – 600.00.

**Trunk-Down Elephant, #2444D.
1922, 5" tall, 5½" wide.
Common. Designer: McDonald.**

Original cost $10.00; recent price range, $450.00 – 550.00; high glaze sets can be found for as little as $250.00. Note size differences.

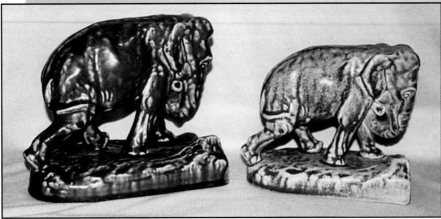

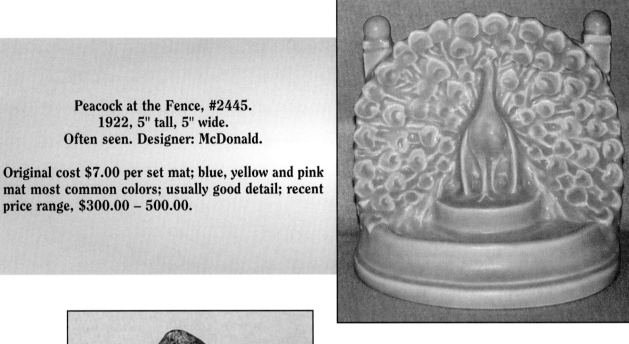

Peacock at the Fence, #2445.
1922, 5" tall, 5" wide.
Often seen. Designer: McDonald.

Original cost $7.00 per set mat; blue, yellow and pink mat most common colors; usually good detail; recent price range, $300.00 – 500.00.

Girl on Bench, #2446.
Left, 1922; right, 1924; 5½" tall, 4" wide.
Often seen. Designer: McDonald.

Original cost $7.00 per set mat; rose, blue and yellow most common colors; many sets will have poor detail in face and hands; recent price range, $300.00 – 450.00.

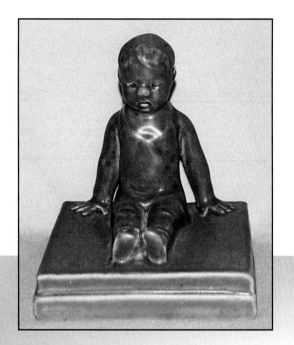
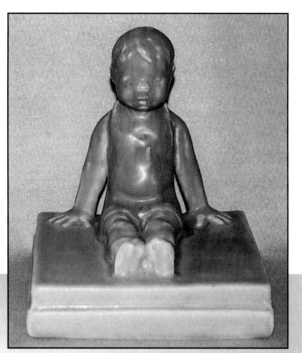

Young Boy, #2447.
Left, 1920; right, 1921; 5½" tall, 5" wide.
Hard to find. Designer: McDonald.

First mold November 1917; best sets have excellent detail in boy's hands and face; original cost $5.00; recent price range, $450.00 – 650.00.

Two Readers on Book, #2502.
1921, 7" tall, 6" wide.
Rare. Designer: Abel.

First appeared in October 1919; original cost $10.00; recent price range, $1,500.00 – 2,500.00.

Sphinx, #2503.
Both 1920; 7" tall, 6" wide.
Hard to find. Designer: Abel.

First mold November 1919; usually little detail in book Sphinx holds, or in paneling on inside back of each bookend; original cost $10.00; recent price range, $800.00 – 1,500.00; well-defined mat examples with good color will easily bring the top end of range.

Egyptian, #2510.
Above, front and back views shown, 1924; below, 1925; 5½" tall, 7" wide.
Hard to find. Designer: McDonald.

Original cost $15.00 mat, $20.00 polychrome; polychrome can be seen in both mat and high glaze; recent price range, $850.00 – 1,300.00.

Reclining Panther, #2564.
1937, 5¾" tall, 7" wide.
Often seen. Designer: McDonald.

Original cost $10.00 per set; look for
early mat glaze, solid colors; high glaze
1940s sets are less desirable; 1930s cost
$12.00 mat, $15.00 porcelain; recent
price range, $400.00 – 750.00, though
one auction price of $1,400.00 has been
recorded.

Double Owls, #2565.
1922, 7" tall, 6" wide.
Hard to find. Designer: McDonald.

Original cost $15.00 in mat; brown and blue
mat seen most frequently; recent price range,
$750.00 – 1,000.00.

Bookends

Kneeling Horse, #2588.
Left, 1922; below, 1923; 5½" tall, 6" wide.
Hard to find. Designer: McDonald.

First mold January 1922; original cost $8.00; recent price range, $900.00 – 1,200.00.

Frog, #2603.
1923, 5" tall, 5¾" wide.
Rare. Designer: Shirayamadani.

First appeared in 1922; recent price range, $1,600.00 – 2,500.00; higher end of range for mat examples, lower end for high glaze.

Pelican, #2614.
1923, 7" tall, 6½" wide.
Rare. Designer: Shirayamadani.

Original cost $10.00; have seen only one example; note the turtle by the feet of pelican; estimated auction value, $2,000.00 – 3,000.00.

Eagle, #2623.
Left, 1928; right, 1945; 6½" tall, 7" wide.
Hard to find. Designer: McDonald.

1920s and 1930s sets are most desirable; 1940s sets often heavily crazed; original cost $15.00; recent price range, $550.00 – 850.00.

Seal, #2642.
1922, 6½" tall, 6½" wide.
Rare. Designer: Shirayamadani.

Original cost $10.00; recent price range, $2,500.00 – 3,500.00.

Pair of Geese, #2651.
Left, 1923; right, 1922; 6" tall, 6½" wide.
Rare. Designer: Shirayamadani.

Original cost $10.00; recent price range, $2,500.00 – 3,000.00.

Small Owl, #2655.
Above left, 1946; 6" tall, 3¾" wide.
Common. Designer: McDonald.

See #2565 for original shape; original cost $5.00; sets rarely have much feather detail; look for unusual mat colors; recent price range, $150.00 – 400.00; lower end of range for high glaze 1940s sets and upper end for mat 1920s and 1930s.

Large Owl, #2656.
1927, 6½" tall, 4" wide.
Hard to find. Designer: McDonald.

See #2565 for original shape; larger size than #2655; much more detail than smaller version; recent price range, $450.00 – 650.00.

Kingfisher, #2657.
Above, 1923; below left, 1939; below right, 1935; 5½" tall, 5" wide.
Often seen. Designer: McDonald.

Original cost $7.00; recent price range, $450.00 – 650.00.

Blackbird, #2658.
Above, 1924; below, 1922; 5½" tall, 5½" wide.
Rare. Designer: Shirayamadani.

Look for repairs on beaks; original cost $7.00; recent price range, $600.00 – 900.00.

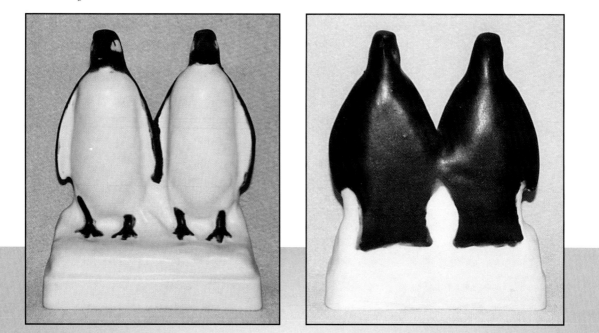

Penguins, #2659.
All 1924; 5½" tall, 4½" wide.
Rare. Designer: Shirayamadani.

May have repaired beaks; original cost, $7.00; available in both polychrome and mat; recent price range, $900.00 – 1,300.00.

Monkey on Books, #2669.
Both 1923; 5½" tall, 5½" wide.
Rare. Designer: Shirayamadani

Have seen only in mat finish; estimated auction value, $1,500.00 – 2,000.00.

Walking Bear, #2678.
Both 1923; 4½" tall, 6½" wide.
Hard to find. Designer: Shirayamadani.

Brown, green, and ivory examples are most often found; original cost $8.00; recent price range, $900.00
– 1,400.00.

Broadside Ship, #2694.
1935, 5½" tall, 5½" wide.
Common. Designer: McDonald.

Blue, brown, or green mat most often seen; look for detail in deck of ship; recent price range, $350.00 – 450.00.

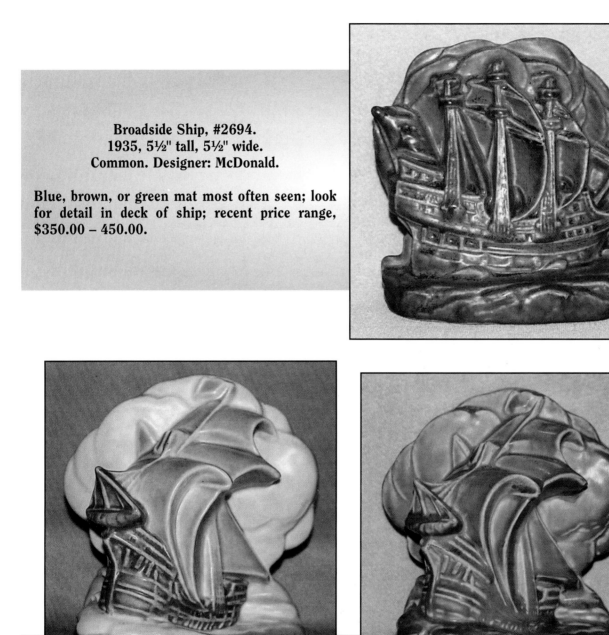

Full Sail Ship, #2695.
Both 1943; 5½" tall, 5½" wide.
Common. Designer: McDonald.

Because of exaggerated three dimensional effect, often has sail chips; original cost $7.00; recent price range, $350.00 – 450.00.

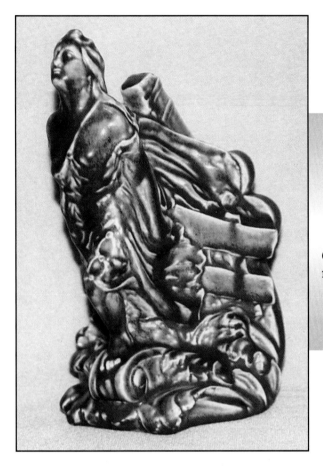

Figurehead, #2732.
1926, 7½" tall, 4½" wide.
Rare. Designer: McDonald.

Original cost $10.00; available both in polychrome and mat; estimated auction value, $3,000.00 – 4,000.00.

Collie Dog, #2778.
1930, 6½" tall, 6" wide.
Often seen. Designer: McDonald.

Frequently has repaired ears; original cost $8.00, later raised to $10.00; recent price range, $500.00 – 750.00.

Jay Bird, #2829.
Above, 1937; below, 1932; 5½" tall, 5" wide.
Hard to find. Designer: Shirayamadani.

Original cost $7.00; recent price range, $400.00 – 600.00.

Water Lilies, #2836.
Above, 1946; below, 1926; 3¾" tall, 5¾" wide.
Common. Designer: unknown.

Original cost $7.00 mat, $12.00 decorated; among the least expensive of bookend sets; recent price range, $150.00 – 400.00; top end of range only seen for polychrome examples.

Basket of Flowers, #2837.
Both 1928; 6" tall, 5¾" wide.
Often seen. Designer: Shirayamadani.

Original cost $7.00 per set for single color mat, $12.00 polychrome; recent price range, $500.00 – 700.00 polychrome, $350.00 – 500.00 for single color.

Beagle Dog, #2998.
1940, 5" tall, 5½" wide.
Common. Designer: Abel.

Best sets have good detail in dog's paws; original cost $10.00; recent price range, $300.00 – 600.00; top end of range for unusual glazes.

Bookends

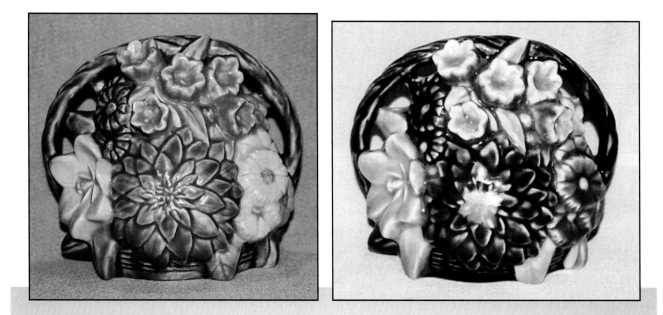

Handled Basket of Flowers, #6001.
Both 1929; 5" tall, 6" wide.
Hard to find. Designer: Shirayamadani.

Original cost $7.00 plain, $12.00 decorated; available both in polychrome and mat; recent price range, $500.00 – 1,000.00; low end of range for solid colors, high end for polychrome.

Horsehead, #6014.
1927, 6" tall, 5½" wide.
Often seen. Designer: McDonald.

Original cost $10.00; recent price range, $500.00 – 750.00; 1940s high glaze sets can be found for $300.00 – 500.00.

Parrot, #6018.
1927, 7¼" tall, 5½" wide.
Rare. Designer: Toohey.

Original cost $10.00 mat, $15.00 polychrome; estimated auction value, $3,000.00 – 3,500.00 for a polychrome set.

Lion, #6019.
Left, 1928; right, 1929; 6½" tall, 4" wide.
Often seen. Designer: Abel.

Rust, green and ivory most common colors; usually little detail; original cost $7.00, porcelain $8.00; recent price range, $600.00 – 1,000.00.

Swan, #6021.
Above, 1928; below, 1929; 4" tall, 5" wide.
Rare. Designer: Toohey.

Original cost $2.50 (unclear as to whether this is for one or a set); most sets are polychrome; recent price range, $750.00 – 1,000.00.

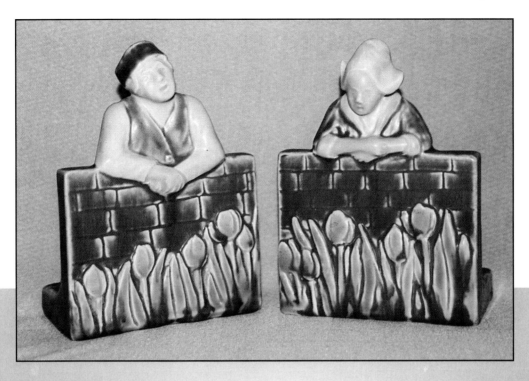

Dutch Boy and Girl, #6022.
Front and back shown. 1928, 6" tall, 4¼" wide.
Often seen. Designer: Toohey.

Original cost $7.00 plain, $12.00 polychrome; most sets we have seen have been polychrome; recent price range, $550.00 – 950.00.

Bookends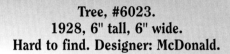

Tree, #6023.
1928, 6" tall, 6" wide.
Hard to find. Designer: McDonald.

Available both in polychrome and mat; original cost $5.00 plain, $7.00 polychrome; recent price range, $650.00 – 1,200.00.

Colonial Lady with Book, #6037.
1929, 6½" tall, 6" wide.
Hard to find. Designer: McDonald.

Often confused with #6252, this set is not nearly so common; original cost $7.00 mat, $12.00 decorated; recent price range, $550.00 – 850.00.

Trunk-Up Elephant, #6124.
1929, 7½" tall, 5" wide.
Often seen. Designer: McDonald.

Original cost $10.00; elephants are one of Rookwood's most often collected animal forms; hence this slightly elevated price for an often seen shape; recent price range, $1,000.00 – 1,500.00 for good mat glaze sets; high glaze or ivory 1940s sets can be found for $400.00 – 800.00.

Eagle, #6139.
1932, 7" tall.
Rare. Designer: Rehm.

Original cost $8.00 mat,
$10.00 porcelain; estimated
auction value, $1,000.00 –
1,500.00.

Man-O-War with Standard, #6140.
1930, 6½" tall, 5½" wide.
Hard to find. Designer: McDonald.

Same shape as #6202 but with standard (brace); original cost
$10.00; recent price range, $800.00 – 1,000.00.

Castle Gate, #6154.
1930, 6" tall.
Rare. Designer: McDonald.

Original cost $7.00; relatively poor detail in known examples; estimated auction value, $3,500.00 – 4,000.00.

Basket of Fruit, #6155.
Year unknown.
Never seen. Designer: Toohey.

Original cost $7.00; estimated auction value, $2,000.00
– 3,000.00.

Bookends

Indian Head, #6158.
1930, 5¾" tall, 5½" wide.
Rare. Designer: McDonald.

Great detail in the one known example; estimated auction value, $3,000.00 – 4,000.00.

Kneeling Female Nude, #6159.
1930, 7" tall, 4" wide.
Rare. Designer: Abel.

Original cost $10.00; recent price range, $2,000.00 – 3,000.00.

Windmill, #6168.
1930, 7" tall, 6" wide.
Rare. Designer: Toohey.

Original cost $7.00 mat single color, $8.00 poly-chrome; estimated auction value, $2,000.00 – 3,000.00.

Man-O-War without Standard, #6202.
Left, 1931; right, 1935; 6¾" tall, 5½" wide.
Hard to find. Designer: McDonald.

Same shape as #6140 but without standard (brace); original cost $10.00; recent price range, $800.00 – 1,000.00 at auction. However, a single, high-glaze example recently sold for more than $1,300.00!

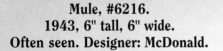

Mule, #6216.
1943, 6" tall, 6" wide.
Often seen. Designer: McDonald.

Original cost $10.00 for set; most often found in ivory mat, but brown and tan also found; many sets will have repaired ears and/or legs; recent price range, $500.00 – 800.00.

Bookends ☀

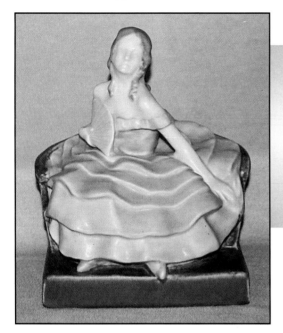

Colonial Woman with Fan, #6252.
1935, 6½" tall, 5½" wide.
Often seen. Designer: McDonald.

Original cost $7.00 per set; available both in polychrome and mat; recent price range, $400.00 – 600.00; high glaze 1940s sets can be found for under $300.00.

Large Elephant, #6256.
1931, 6½" tall, 7½" wide.
Rare. Designer: Abel.

Original cost $7.00; because of size may have been sold as a figural; estimated auction value, $2,000.00 – 3,000.00 for a set.

Fish, #6259.
1931, 6" tall, 7" wide.
Rare. Designer: Shirayamadani.

Original cost $7.00; estimated auction value, $1,500.00 – 2,000.00.

Seated Elephant, #6261.
1931, 5½" tall, 5½" wide.
Rare. Designer: Shirayamadani.

Original cost $8.00 per set; estimated auction value,
$1,500.00 – 2,000.00.

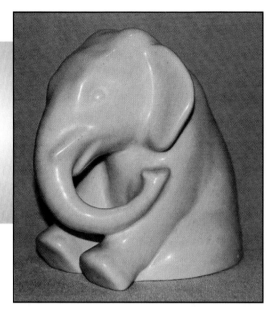

Bird, #6323.
7" tall.
Never seen. Designer: Shirayamadani.

Estimated auction value, $2,000.00 – 3,000.00.

Owl, #6324.
8¾" tall.
Never seen. Designer: Shirayamadani.

Estimated auction value, $2,000.00 – 3,000.00.

Bookends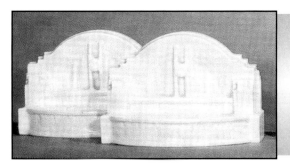

Union Terminal, #6378.
1933, 4½" tall.
Rare. Designer: Conant.

Original cost $10.00; this representation of Cincinnati's famous train station is one of the most sought-after sets of bookends; recent price range, $5,000.00 – 7,500.00.

Hippopotamus, #6384.
1933, 4½" tall, 6½" wide.
Hard to find. Designer: Conant.

First made August 1933; original cost $7.00; usually seen in mat ivory; recent price range, $1,500.00 – 2,000.00.

Rooster, #6386.
1933, 7" tall, 6½" wide.
Rare. Designer: Conant.

Original cost $7.00; estimated auction value, $2,000.00 – 3,000.00.

 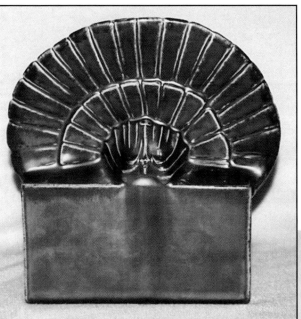

Turkey, #6417.
Front and back shown. 1933, 5½" tall, 6" wide, 4" deep.
Rare. Designer: Conant.

Original cost $7.00; estimated auction value, $2,000.00 – 3,000.00.

Deer, #6447.
1934, 4½" tall, 5" wide.
Rare. Designer: Conant.

Original cost $7.00; first mold May 1934; estimated auction value, $2,000.00 – 3,000.00.

Scottie Dog, #6449.
Above left, 1937; above right, 1958; below, 1937; 5" tall, 5" wide.
Hard to find. Designer: Conant.

Original cost $5.00; recent price range, $500.00 – 900.00.

Flying Fish, #6482.
1934, 4" tall, 6" wide.
Rare. Designer: Abel.

Original cost $5.00; estimated auction value,
$1,000.00 – 1,500.00.

Seated Polar Bear, #6484.
1934, 4½" tall, 5" wide.
Hard to find. Designer: Abel.

Original cost $7.00; available with and without blackened
eyes; recent price range, $2,000.00 – 2,500.00.

Honey Bear, #6485.
1948, 4½" tall, 6" wide.
Rare. Designer: Abel.

Original cost $7.00; recent price range, $2,500.00 – 3,500.00.

Bookends

Eagle on Platform, #6491.
1945, 5½" tall, 8" wide.
Often seen. Designer: Abel.

Original cost $15.00 mat; recent price range, $500.00 – 1,000.00.

Monkey without Base, #6501.
1935, 5" tall, 5" wide.
Hard to find. Designer: Abel.

Original cost $7.00; recent price range, $600.00 – 1,000.00.

Lotus, #6508.
1945, 4" tall, 6" wide.
Often seen. Designer: Shirayamadani.

Original cost $5.00; recent price range, $300.00 – 400.00.

Bird, #6519.
5½" tall.
Never seen. Designer: Shirayamadani.

Estimated auction value, $2,000.00 – 3,000.00.

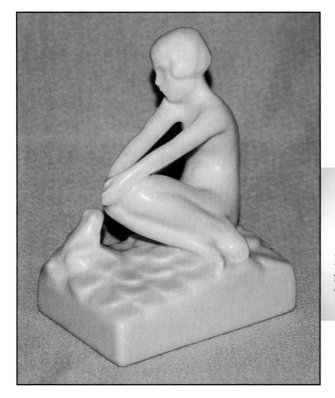

Seated Nude with Frog, #6521.
1935, 4½" tall, 3½" wide.
Often seen. Designer: Abel.

First mold April 1935; original cost $6.00; this may really be a paperweight; recent price range, $500.00 – 750.00.

Small Arrangement of Fruit, #6580.
1939, 4½" tall, 5" wide.
Rare. Designer: Shirayamadani.

Original cost $5.00; estimated auction value, $900.00 – 1,500.00, but good polychrome sets could exceed top limit.

Bookends

Chow Dog, #6584.
1940, 8" tall, 7½" wide.
Rare. Designer: Brown.

Original cost $10.00 plain for a single; $18.00 for set; could be classified as a bookend or as an animal figural; recent price range, $1,400.00 – 2,000.00.

Sunflower and Ladybug, #6594.
Left and below, 1937, 4" tall, 5½" wide.
Rare. Designer: Shirayamadani.

Estimated auction value, $3,000.00 – 4,000.00 for polychrome.

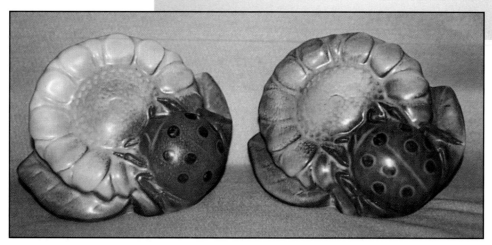

Three Pelicans, #6627.
Year unknown.
Never seen. Designer: Shirayamadani.

Estimated auction value, $2,000.00 – 3,000.00.

Three Blind Mice, #6641.
Right and below, 1937; 4" tall, 4¼" wide.
Rare. Designer: Shirayamadani.

Original cost $5.00; recent price range, $1,750.00 –
2,500.00.

Bookends

Double Donkeys, #6697.
1937, 4½" tall.
Rare. Designer: Shirayamadani.

Original cost $5.00; embossed on base "When Shall We Three Meet Again"; recent price range, $1,850.00 – 2,500.00.

Giraffe, #6768.
Both 1940; 5" tall, 6½" wide.
Hard to find. Designer: Abel.

Usually seen in ivory mat or two-tone brown; recent price range, $1,750.00 – 2,500.00.

Cacti, #6787.
1941, 4½" tall, 5" wide.
Rare. Designer: Shirayamadani.

Estimated auction value, $1,000.00 – 2,000.00.

St. Francis, #6883.
1945, 7½" tall, 5" wide.
Often seen. Designer: Zanetta.

This and #2998 are most common bookend forms in the 1940s; usually found in polychrome; recent price range, $650.00 – 900.00.

Angel, #6897.
1945, 7" tall, 5" wide.
Rare. Designer: Zanetta.

Most examples dated 1945 or 1946; high glaze, and may be heavily crazed; recent price range, $1,000.00 – 2,000.00.

Sleeping Man, #7115.
Three angles shown. 1953, 8" tall, 5½" wide.
Rare. Designer: Hentschel.

Unidentified in Peck's book. Must have been designed by Hentschel before he left Rookwood in the mid-1930s; estimated auction value, $2,000.00 – 2,500.00.

The Hebrew Union College, Special.
Front and back shown. 1948, 6¼" tall, 4¾" wide.
Hard to find. Designer: unknown.

Thought to have been a donor's gift for the 75th anniversary of Cincinnati's Hebrew Union College in 1950; recent price range, $2,000.00 – 2,500.00.

PAPERWEIGHTS

The first reference we find to a Rookwood paperweight is from a desk set produced in 1894. The first separately numbered paperweight is the Owl, shape #1084, initially molded in 1904. As we pointed out in the previous section, bookends offered Rookwood the potential for attracting new customers, and they were significantly less expensive to produce than were artist-decorated vases, the mainstay of the Rookwood inventory of the time. Much the same can be said for paperweights.

Although a few paperweight shapes were introduced in the period between 1900 and 1925, production really escalated just prior to and just after the Great Depression of 1929. Roughly two of every three paperweights produced by Rookwood appeared after 1927. Our rationalization of this trend is that Rookwood significantly increased their reliance on paperweights to survive the 1930s because of these factors:

1. They were inexpensive to produce, and, therefore, could be offered to customers for considerably less money than vases. Customers of the time had little extra money to spend.

2. Compared to decorated vases, they were less likely to suffer damage during the firing process. Therefore, overhead was lower.

3. Most Rookwood decorators were "let go" after the Depression. In order to keep the showroom stocked, molded items were required.

This compilation includes 83 numbered paperweight shapes and six special paperweight shapes. All shapes called paperweights on the original Rookwood shape cards are included. In addition, we have called the Woman Carrying Pails, #1854, a paperweight, as she stands on a base that resembles a paperweight base and is of a size consistent with other paperweights. Mask, #6662, is included because David Seyler (the designer) told us he intended it to be a paperweight, although it is not so labeled in the shape records. Cocker Spaniel, #7024, resembles the Winking Dog paperweight, #6161, in both shape and size, so we have called it a paperweight rather than an animal figural.

The moment of temporary insanity that allowed us to calculate an approximate cost for a complete set of bookends lingered long enough for us to make a similar calculation for paperweights. The collector of all 89 paperweights would pay $4,000.00 – 6,000.00 for the 16 common shapes, $5,000.00 – 7,000.00 for the 17 often seen shapes, $13,000.00 – 15,000.00 for the 27 hard-to-find shapes, $13,000.00 – 15,000.00 for the 23 rare shapes, and $5,000.00 – 7,000.00 for the six shapes we have never seen (assuming they would appear for sale). Total cost would then be $40,000 – 50,000.

Guide to Paperweights

Desk Set, #755.
1904, ¾" tall, 4¾" wide, 2½" deep.
Rare. Designer: Shreve & Company.

Earliest paperweight mentioned; example in this photo is not marked with shape #755, but is an early weight and of the same dimensions as described in the shape records; estimated auction value, $200.00 – 300.00, although a polychrome example with grape and leaf motif recently brought more than $500.00.

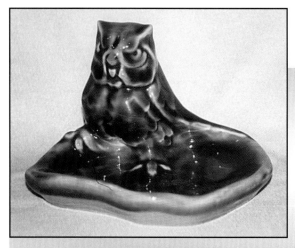

Owl, #1084.
1943, 4½" tall, 7" wide.
Common. Designer: unknown.

Really an ashtray? Might better fit the miscellaneous shapes section; bottom photo shows this paperweight in comparison with its precursor shape, Owl Ashtray #683Z, from the miscellaneous section; original cost $4.00 mat; recent price range, $250.00 – 400.00.

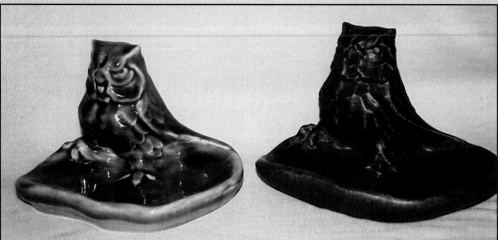

Frog, #1233.
1915, 3½" tall, 5" wide.
Rare. Designer: unknown.

Original cost $2.00; with base; usually seen with dark mat finishes, but one with green high glaze has appeared; later version had a pencil groove on base in front of frog; recent price range, $600.00 – 900.00, although an especially desirable example recently brought $1,600.00.

Rook, #1623.
Right, 1928; below, 1922.
3" tall, 4½" wide.
Common. Designer: Toohey.

First made in 1908; with base; original cost $2.00; collector will have wide choice of color and finish; recent price range, $300.00 – 500.00.

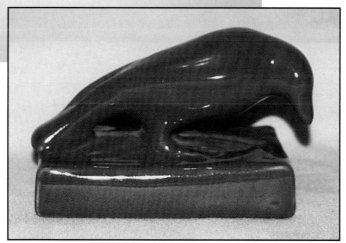

Turtle, #1686.
1910, 2½" tall, 5" wide.
Often seen. Designer: Toohey.

Early mat examples are most valuable; usually seen in darker colors like brown and blue; with base; original cost $2.00 mat; recent price range, $300.00 – 500.00.

Swan, #1696.
Above, 1909; left, 1915; 2½" tall, 5" wide.
Rare. Designer: Shirayamadani.

First mold July 1909; original cost $3.50; with base; neither of the two examples (one mat and one high glaze porcelain) we have seen was well defined; estimated auction value, $400.00 – 600.00.

Woman Carrying Pails, #1854.
1911, 6" tall, 3¾" wide.
Hard to find. Designer: Pons.

First mold December 1910; with base; original cost $2.00; have seen both mat and high glaze examples; recent price range, $300.00 – 500.00.

Geese, #1855.
1927, 4½" tall, 5" wide.
Common. Designer: Toohey.

First mold December 1910; with base; original cost $2.50; recent price range, $250.00 – 400.00.

Cat, #1883.
Left, 1930; right, 1940; 5½" tall, 4" wide.
Hard to find. Designer: Hentschel.

First mold April 1911; usually seen mat; with base; original cost $2.50; recent price range, $450.00 – 750.00.

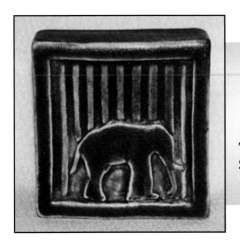

Elephant, #2055.
1914, 2¾" square, 1" tall.
Rare. Designer: unknown.

Tile-like square; original cost $1.00 mat; estimated auction value, $300.00 – 500.00.

Rabbit, #2056.
1921, 2¾" square, 1" tall.
Rare. Designer: unknown.

Tile-like square; original cost $1.00 mat; estimated auction value, $300.00 – 500.00.

Crow, #2057.
1921, 2¾" square, 1" tall.
Rare. Designer: unknown.

Tile-like square; original cost $1.00 mat; estimated auction value, $300.00 – 500.00.

Squirrel, #2058.
2¾" square, 1" tall.
Never seen. Designer: unknown.

Tile-like square; original cost $1.00 mat; estimated auction value, $300.00 – 500.00.

Slipper, #2461.
Year unknown.
Never seen. Designer: Conant.

Rookwood shape card has an "X" drawn through picture, perhaps indicating this shape was never put into production; with base; estimated auction value, $1,000.00 – 1,500.00.

Elephant, #2628.
1922, 3¾" tall, 4¼" wide.
Hard to find. Designer: McDonald.

Has clowns molded on either side of elephant's head; with base; recent price range, $350.00 – 600.00.

Monkey, #2677.
1927, 4" tall, 4¼" wide.
Hard to find. Designer: Shirayamadani.

With base; recent price range, $400.00 – 750.00.

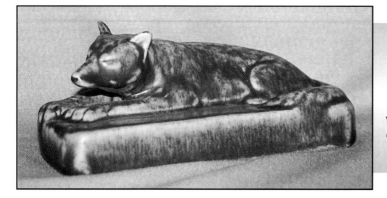

Fox, #2679.
1930, 2½" tall, 5½" wide.
Hard to find. Designer: Shirayamadani.

With base; recent price range, $500.00 – 700.00.

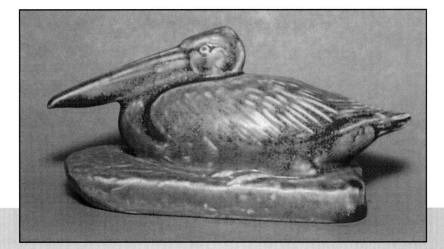

Pelican, #2711.
Above, 1932; below, 1965; 3" tall, 6" wide.
Often seen. Designer: Shirayamadani.

Bill was cast separately, then connected to rest of piece; original cost $2.00; with base; recent price range, $300.00 – 500.00.

Paperweights

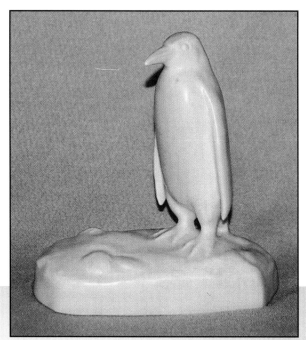

Penguin, #2727.
Left, 1935; right, 1934; 5¼" tall, 5" wide.
Hard to find. Designer: Shirayamadani.

With base; recent price range, $350.00 – 600.00.

Foo Dog, #2747.
1924, 4" tall, 4½" wide.
Hard to find. Designer: Shirayamadani.

Part of a desk set; with base; recent price range, $350.00 – 500.00.

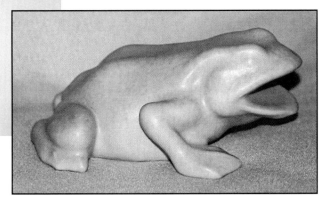

Frog, #2756.
Above, 1930; right, 1929; 2" tall, 4" wide.
Rare. Designer: Shirayamadani.

Without base; original cost $2.50; estimated auction
value, $400.00 – 600.00.

Dog, #2777.
1929, 5" tall, 3½" wide.
Common. Designer: McDonald.

One of the most frequently seen paperweights; with base;
original cost $2.50; recent price range, $200.00 – 300.00.

Paperweights

Ship, #2792.
1932, 4" tall, 3½" wide.
Common. Designer: McDonald.

Original cost $2.00; frequent damage, especially to ship spires; with base; recent price range, $250.00 – 500.00.

Seahorse, #2796.
1927, 3" tall, 4" wide.
Hard to find. Designer: McDonald.

With base; recent price range, $600.00 – 800.00.

Elephant, #2797.
Left, 1925; below, 1930; 3½" tall, 4" wide.
Common. Designer: McDonald.

With base; recent price range, $250.00 – 500.00.

Rook with Acorn, #2810.
Above left, 1924; above right, 1925; below, 1930; 4¼" tall, 5" wide.
Hard to find. Designer: Shirayamadani.

Undervalued in marketplace relative to #2921; with base; recent price range, $400.00 – 600.00.

Paperweights

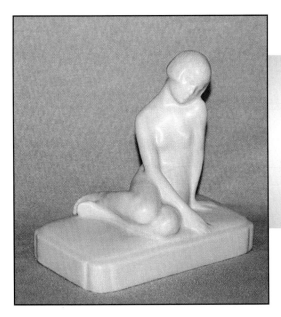

Nude, #2868.
1935, 4½" tall, 4½" wide.
Common. Designer: Abel.

Among the most common of paperweights; original cost $2.50; with base; part of desk set but also sold separately; recent price range, $150.00 – 350.00.

Rookwood Fine Tiles, #2921.
1926, 4" tall, 4½" wide.
Often seen. Designer: Shirayamadani.

One of the most sought-after paperweights; back side of base reads "Fine Tiles"; nearly always seen in mat, with darker colors such as black, blue, and green; recent price range, $1,000.00 – 2,000.00.

Dancer, #2945.
1928, 5" tall, 3" wide.
Rare. Designer: Abel.

See shape #2538; this paperweight is identical to the dancing figure atop the flower holder; estimated auction value, $500.00 – 700.00.

Basket, #6020.
Left, 1928; right, 1927; 3½" tall, 4½" wide.
Hard to find. Designer: Toohey.

Without base; original cost $2.00 mat; seen in polychrome more frequently than single color, usually high glaze rather than mat; recent price range, $300.00 – 500.00, higher end of range for polychrome.

Squirrel, #6025.
Both 1928; 4½" tall, 4" wide.
Hard to find. Designer: Toohey.

Original cost $2.50 plain, $3.00 polychrome; decorated much less common than plain; with base; recent price range, $350.00 – 550.00, although mat ivory examples can be found for $200.00 – 300.00.

Rooster, #6030.
Above left, 1952; above right, 1946; 5¼" tall, 3¼" wide.
Common. Designer: McDonald.

With base; original cost $2.50 plain, $3.00 polychrome; most often found in polychrome, favorite for decoration by junior artists; composite photo below emphasizes the wide range of decorations from which the collector can choose; recent price range, $250.00 – 500.00.

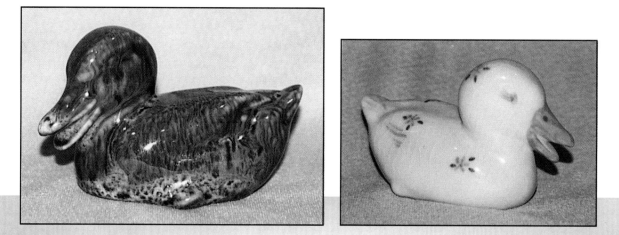

Duck, #6064.
Left, 1964; right, 1945; 2½" tall, 3½" wide.
Common. Designer: Shirayamadani.

Original cost $1.50; usually among the least expensive paperweights; without base; recent price range, $125.00 – 250.00.

Cat, #6065.
Above left and right, 1927; right, 1945; 2¾" tall, 4" wide.
Hard to find. Designer: Shirayamadani.

Without base; occasionally seen decorated but more often plain; recent price range, $400.00 – 700.00.

Fish, #6070.
1928, 2½" tall, 5" wide.
Rare. Designer: Shirayamadani.

Without base; recent price range, $600.00 – 800.00.

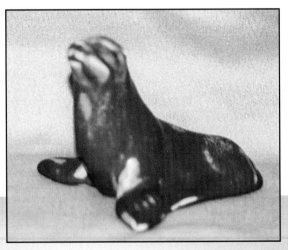

Seal, #6071.
Above left and right, 1929; left, 1928; 3" tall, 4" wide.
Rare. Designer: Shirayamadani.

Without base; recent price range, $600.00 – 1,000.00.

Monkey, #6084.
1929, 4" tall, 2¾" wide.
Hard to find. Designer: Shirayamadani.

Without base; original cost $2.00; recent price range, $250.00 – 400.00.

Gazelle, #6156.
1930, 4¾" tall, 4" wide.
Often seen. Designer: Abel.

Seated; with base; original cost $2.50; recent price range, $200.00 – 400.00.

Paperweights

Rabbit, #6160.
Left, 1960; right, 1946; 3¾" tall, 3½" wide.
Common. Designer: Abel.

Without base; original cost $1.50; recent price range, $150.00 – 250.00, sometimes seen decorated which might elevate price to $300.00 – 400.00.

Dog, #6161.
Both 1930; 4½" tall, 3½" wide.
Rare. Designer: Toohey.

Sometimes called "Winking Dog"; without base; original cost $2.00; recent price range, $400.00 – 700.00.

Chick, #6169.
Left, 1930; right, 1937; 4" tall, 3" wide.
Hard to find. Designer: Abel.

With base; original cost $1.50; usually seen in ivory mat, occasionally yellow mat; recent price range, $300.00 – 500.00, although an example recently sold for $850.00.

Goat, #6170.
1937, 6½" tall, 4¾" wide.
Common. Designer: Abel.

Among most common of paperweights; with base; original cost $2.50; recent price range, $150.00 – 250.00.

Beagle, #6172.
1937, 3½" tall, 5" wide.
Hard to find. Designer: Abel.

Original cost $2.00; without base; figural looks more like dachshund than beagle (reasonable considering Abel's German ancestry); recent price range, $350.00 – 550.00.

Cat, #6182.
Left, 1946; center, 1943; right, 1935; 6½" tall, 5½" wide.
Hard to find. Designer: Abel.

Almost always seen in high glaze; without base; original cost $4.00; recent price range, $400.00 – 700.00 for high glaze examples; a rare mat example in an attractive brown glaze recently sold for over $800.00, and a few sales of over $1,000.00 have been recorded for unusually good high glaze examples.

Donkey, #6241.
1931, 6" tall, 4½" wide.
Often seen. Designer: Abel.

With base; original cost $3.00; recent price range,
$200.00 – 400.00.

Parrot, #6242.
1931, 8½" tall, 4½" wide.
Rare. Designer: Abel.

Have seen only one; with base; original cost $5.00; esti-
mated auction value, $600.00 – 800.00.

Fabeltier, #6243.
Left, 1931; right, 1934; 4¼" tall, 5" wide.
Often seen. Designer: Abel.

Original cost $2.00; nice with double glazes; without base; recent price range, $300.00 – 500.00.

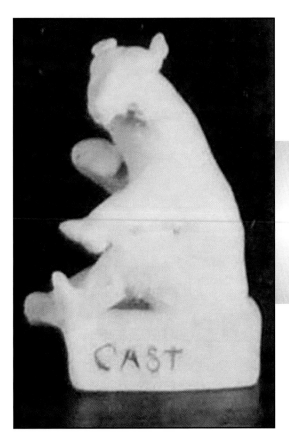

Bear, #6273.
Year unknown.
Never seen. Designer: McDonald.

With base; estimated auction value, $1,000.00 – 2,000.00.

Woodpecker, #6277.
1931, 4¾" tall, 6¼" wide.
Hard to find.
Designer: Shirayamadani.

Without base; recent price range,
$400.00 – 600.00.

Snail, #6285.
Front and back shown, 1931; 3" tall, 5" wide.
Rare. Designer: Abel.

We've only seen one! Estimated auction value,
$2,000.00 – 2,500.00.

Paperweights

Pelican, #6328.
1936, 5" tall, 3" wide.
Hard to find. Designer: Shirayamadani.

With base; recent price range, $300.00 – 450.00.

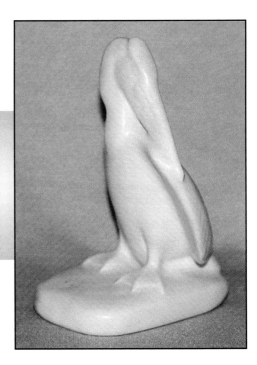

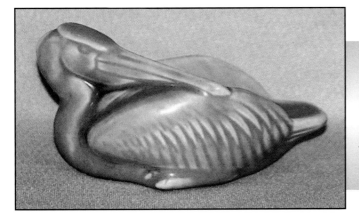

Pelican, #6329.
1932, 2½" tall, 4½" wide.
Often seen. Designer: Shirayamadani.

First mold May 1932; possibly tray or pin tray; without base; recent price range, $150.00 – 300.00.

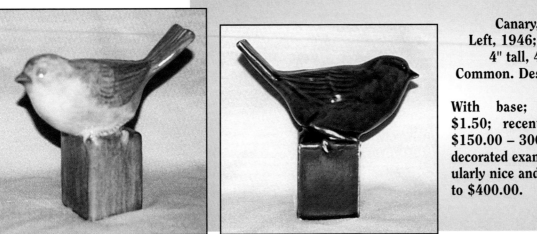

Canary, #6383.
Left, 1946; right, 1940;
4" tall, 4¼" wide.
Common. Designer: Conant.

With base; original cost $1.50; recent price range, $150.00 – 300.00, but artist-decorated examples are particularly nice and could bring up to $400.00.

Apple, #6385.
1935, 3" tall, 3" wide.
Often seen. Designer: Shirayamadani.

Without base; recent price range, $100.00 – 200.00.

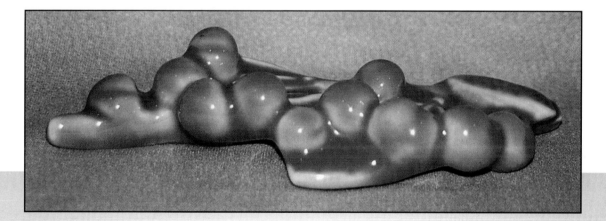

Cherries, #6388.
1933, 1" tall, 6" wide.
Often seen. Designer: Shirayamadani.

First mold 1933; without base; recent price range, $100.00 – 200.00.

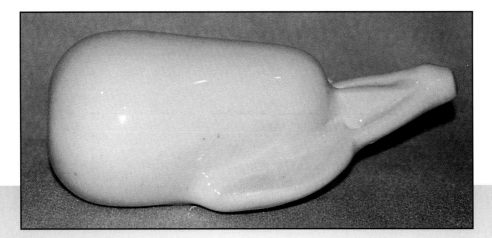

Pear, #6389.
1933, 2" tall, 5" wide.
Often seen. Designer: Shirayamadani.

First mold 1933; without base; recent price range, $100.00 – 200.00.

Peaches, #6394.
1933, 2" tall, 6" wide.
Often seen. Designer: Shirayamadani.

Without base; original cost $1.50; recent price range, $100.00 – 200.00.

Cat, #6402.
Left, 1964; right, 1965; 4¾" tall, 3" wide.
Hard to find. Designer: Conant.

Prices for this shape have escalated recently; with base; original cost $1.50; recent price range, $600.00 – 1,000.00.

Donkey, #6404.
1934, 4" tall, 5½" wide.
Hard to find. Designer: Conant.

With baskets; frequently referred to by collectors as the "Burro" to differentiate from Donkey #6241; with base; original cost $3.00; recent price range, $250.00 – 450.00.

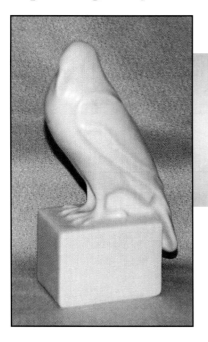

Hawk, #6405.
1936, 4½" tall, 3" wide.
Rare. Designer: Conant.

With base; original cost $1.50; recent price range, $450.00 – 650.00.

Mandarin Duck, #6409.
1933, 2½" tall, 3" wide.
Often seen. Designer: Conant.

With base; often found in ivory mat; original cost $1.50;
recent price range, $300.00 – 400.00.

Monkey, #6426.
1935, 5" tall, 3¼" wide.
Hard to find. Designer: Shirayamadani.

With base; recent price range, $300.00 – 500.00.

Rose, #6437.
1940, 1½" tall, 3¾" wide.
Common. Designer: Shirayamadani.

Without base; original cost $1.50; recent price range,
$100.00 – 200.00.

Pelican, #6439.
1934, 5¼" tall, 3" wide.
Rare. Designer: Conant.

With tapered base; original cost $1.50; recent price range,
$600.00 – 800.00.

Easter Lily, #6441.
Year unknown.
Never seen. Designer: Shirayamadani.

Without base; original cost $1.50; estimated auction value,
$500.00 – 700.00.

Goose, #6446.
1939, 5" tall, 4" wide.
Rare. Designer: Conant.

With base; original cost $2.00; recent price range, $300.00 – 500.00.

Reclining Bulldog, #6481.
1934, 3" tall, 5" wide.
Hard to find. Designer: Abel.

Memorializes "Butch," E.T. Hurley's dog; without base; original cost $2.50; most often seen in white high glaze; recent price range, $350.00 – 650.00.

Bulldog, #6483.
Left, 1943; below, 1946; 5" tall, 4½" wide.
Hard to find. Designer: Abel.

Sitting on haunches; often found polychrome; without base; original cost $3.50 plain, $5.00 polychrome; sometimes found with "Butch" impressed on base — after E.T. Hurley's dog; recent price range, $600.00 – 1,000.00.

Elephant, #6488.
1945, 4" tall, 4" wide.
Hard to find. Designer: Conant.

Characterized by long ears and indented base; original cost $2.00; recent price range, $250.00 – 500.00.

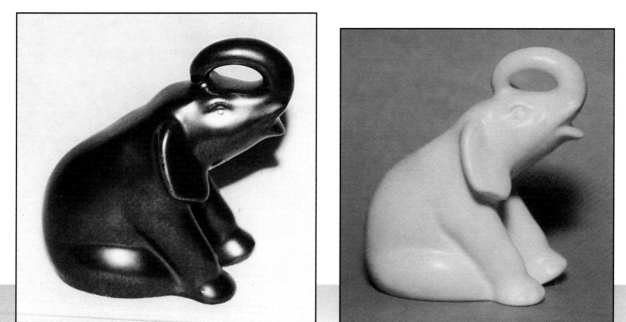

Elephant, #6490.
Left, 1951; right, 1947; 4" tall, 4" wide.
Often seen. Designer: Shirayamadani.

Trunk up; without base; original cost $1.50; recent price range, $200.00 – 400.00.

Gazelle, #6528.
1936, 5" tall, 4" wide.
Hard to find. Designer: Brown.

First mold May 1935; with base; original cost $3.00 and
$3.50; recent price range, $500.00 – 750.00.

Ladybug, #6595.
1936, 1½" tall, 3½" wide, 3" deep.
Rare. Designer: Shirayamadani.

Original cost $2.50; inscribed on base "Ladybug, Ladybug, fly away
home; Your house is on fire your children are gone. All but one and
her name is Anne, And she crept under the pudding pan"; estimated
auction value, $2,000.00 – 3,000.00.

Mouse, #6618.
1937, 3½" tall, 3" wide.
Rare. Designer: Shirayamadani.

As the story goes, Shirayamadani fashioned this mouse after a "pet" of
his that cleaned up the crumbs from his noon lunch site every day; with
base; original cost $1.50; recent price range, $600.00 – 1,000.00.

Paperweights

Bunnies, #6643.
1958, 3½" tall, 3½" wide.
Rare. Designer: Shirayamadani.

One bunny standing, one sitting; without base; estimated auction value, $600.00 – 1,000.00.

Kitten, #6661.
1943, 1½" tall, 3½" wide.
Hard to find. Designer: Seyler.

Lying on back; without base; original cost $1.50; recent price range, $400.00 – 900.00.

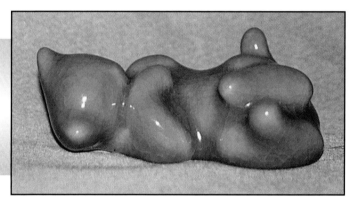

Mask, #6662.
1937, 3½" tall, 2½" wide.
Rare. Designer: Seyler.

Without base; not listed as paperweight by Rookwood, but Seyler considered it to be one; estimated auction value, $400.00 – 600.00.

Reclining Lamb, #6663.
1939, 3" tall, 5" wide.
Hard to find. Designer: Seyler.

With base; original cost $2.00; recent
price range, $300.00 – 500.00.

Mother and Child, #6664.
1938, 6" tall.
Rare. Designer: Seyler.

Without base; estimated auction value, $500.00 – 800.00.

Standing Lamb, #6665.
1959, 5" tall, 4½" wide.
Common. Designer: Seyler.

Among most common of paperweights; without base; original cost $2.50; recent price range, $175.00 – 300.00.

Fat Fairy, #6667.
1937, 5" tall, 4" wide.
Rare. Designer: Seyler.

First mold September 1937; we have seen only one of these; with base; estimated auction value, $400.00 – 600.00.

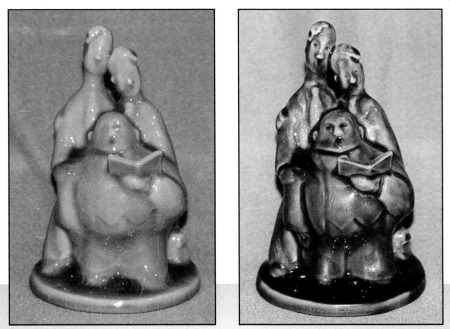

Radio Singers, #6683.
Left, 1948; right, 1937; 5" tall, 3½" wide.
Often seen. Designer: Seyler.

Usually seen in wine madder glaze; with base; original cost $3.50; recent price range, $200.00 – 400.00.

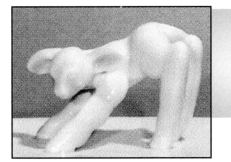

Calf, #6809.
1943, 4" tall, 5" wide.
Rare. Designer: unknown.

Without base; estimated auction value, $500.00 – 800.00.

Cocker Spaniel, #7024.
1953, 4½" tall, 4" wide.
Common. Designer: possibly Wareham.

Model was a gift to Wareham; without base; left foot up; recent price range, $250.00 – 400.00.

Harvard Second Triennial, Special.
1905, 1" tall, 5" wide, 3" deep.
Rare. Designer: unknown.

Inscription on top "Veritas, Harvard 99 Second Triennial, 1905"; recent price range, $200.00 – 300.00.

Open Book, Special.
1924, 1" tall, 3¾" wide, 1½" deep.
Often seen. Designer: unknown.

Inscribed on base, "Reunion Commercial Club of Boston-Chicago-Cincinnati-St. Louis, White Sulfur Springs, W. Va. May 30 – June 1, 1924"; recent price range, $200.00 – 300.00.

CWBC, Special.
1949, 3" diameter, ½" tall.
Often seen. Designer: unknown.

Made only in 1949; recent price range, $75.00 – 150.00.

Potter at the Wheel, Special.
1948, 4" diameter, ½" tall.
Often seen. Designer: unknown.

Inscribed on base, "Potter at the Wheel, Rookwood, Cincinnati, Ohio"; often seen with poor mold definition; recent price range, $75.00 – 200.00; higher end of range seen for those examples with better mold definition.

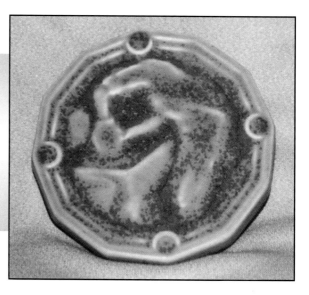

B.P.O.E. Elk, #763Z.
1904, 4" diameter, 1" tall.
Rare. Designer: unknown.

Made in 1904 for Elk's Club celebration; recent price range, $200.00 – 300.00.

Butchers' Supply, Special.
1949, 3½" diameter, 1" tall.
Often seen. Designer: unknown.

Advertising piece made for the Cincinnati Butchers' Supply Company; recent price range, $100.00 – 300.00.

ANIMAL FIGURALS

Most of the animal-related shapes designed and sold by Rookwood were functional — bookends and paperweights have already been reviewed, while candleholders, trays, etc., will be covered in the next section. A few are non-functional and don't fit in any of these categories. We have chosen to call these shapes "figurals," as they are purely decorative rather than functional.

This compilation includes 22 numbered animal figural shapes and one special animal figural shape. All animal figurals not labeled as paperweights, bookends, or miscellaneous shapes on the original Rookwood shape cards are included. However, we have chosen to exclude a few of the very last Rookwood shapes, numbers above 7175, because the images on the shape cards are so nondescript that positive identification becomes nearly impossible.

Guide to Animal Figurals

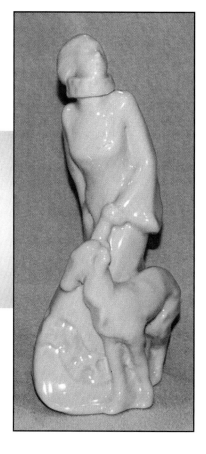

Woman with Dog, #2290.
1916, 9½" tall, 4½" wide.
Rare. Designer: Haswell.

Original cost $7.00 porcelain; recent price range, $500.00 – 700.00.

Leopard, #2563.
Above: 1930; right: 1945;
3½" tall, 6½" wide.
Often seen. Designer: McDonald.

Recent price range, $400.00 – 700.00.

Swan, #2601.
Year unknown.
Never seen. Designer: Shirayamadani.

This shape is called a Swan in the original Rookwood records, and is shown with the extended beak. Did Rookwood realize before the shape was put into production that swans have shorter beaks? Is this the reason the shape has not (to our knowledge) been seen? Estimated auction value, $400.00 – 600.00.

Crow, #2636.
1922, 10" tall, 9½" wide.
Rare. Designer: McDonald.

Often called "Large Rook" but original shape card calls it "Crow"; recent price range, $1,500.00 – 2,000.00.

Pheasant, #2832.
1946, 9" tall, 13" wide.
Often seen. Designer: Shirayamadani.

Usually polychrome; recent price range, $300.00 – 600.00.

Camel, #6166.
1930, 8½" tall, 6¾" wide.
Rare. Designer: Abel.

Without lid; original cost $10.00
mat, $12.00 porcelain; recent price
range, $1,500.00 – 2,000.00.

Scottie Dog, #6278.
1931, 6" tall, 8" wide.
Rare. Designer: Abel.

See shape #6279 for Scottie Dog with lid; original cost $6.00; estimated auction value, $2,000.00 – 3,000.00.

Scottie Dog, #6279.
1931, 6" tall, 8" wide.
Rare. Designer: Abel.

With lid; original cost $7.00; see shape #6278 for Scottie Dog without lid; estimated auction value, $2,000.00 – 3,000.00.

Camel, #6297.
1931, 6" tall, 7½" wide.
Rare. Designer: Abel.

With lid; see shape #6166 for camel without lid; note that they are different sizes; estimated auction value, $1,500.00 – 2,500.00.

Sailor on Horseback, #6698.
7½" tall.
Never seen. Designer: Seyler.

Original cost $10.00; estimated auction value, $500.00 – 1,000.00.

Bird, #6780.
1940, 6½" tall, 6½" wide.
Often seen. Designer: Shirayamadani.

Usually polychrome; original cost $3.50 mat, $10.00 polychrome; recent price range, $250.00 – 400.00.

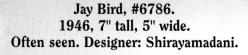

Jay Bird, #6786.
1946, 7" tall, 5" wide.
Often seen. Designer: Shirayamadani.

Usually polychrome; original cost $10.00; recent price range, $250.00 – 400.00.

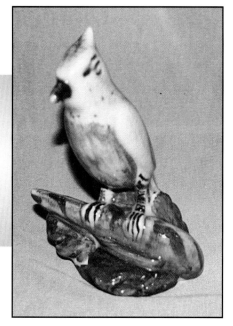

Fisherman, #6808.
1942, 9½" tall, 4¾" wide.
Rare. Designer: Reich.

The two examples we have seen have had different colors for shoes, suspenders, and fish; incised on base "J. Reich, 1942"; estimated auction value, $700.00 – 1,000.00.

Bird, #6837.
Both 1946; 5" tall, 6" wide.
Often seen. Designer: Shirayamadani.

Usually polychrome; original cost $3.50, $5.00, or $7.50, depending on decoration; recent price range, $250.00 – 400.00.

Parrot on a Perch, #6842.
1943, 13" tall, 5" wide.
Rare. Designer: Shirayamadani.

Original cost $12.00; Peck incorrectly lists this bird as a cockatoo; recent price range, $800.00 – 1,200.00.

Cockatoo, #6843.
1943, 10" tall, 5" wide.
Hard to find. Designer: Shirayamadani.

First mold February 1943; usually polychrome; original cost
$7.00 one color, $10.00 polychrome; recent price range,
$300.00 – 600.00.

Carousel Horse, #6929.
1946, 8½" tall, 5" wide.
Hard to find. Designer: Rehm.

Usually found in white, high glaze; recent price range,
$300.00 – 500.00.

Animal Figurals

Pigeon, #6930.
Above, 1959; below, 1945;
2½" tall, 7" wide.
Rare. Designer: Ley.

Estimated auction value, $300.00 – 500.00.

Parrot, #6954.
1946, 12" tall, 7" wide.
Rare. Designer: Zanetta.

Estimated auction value, $600.00 – 1,000.00
for solid color, $1,000.00 – 1,500.00 for
polychrome.

Egret, #6972.
1950, 9½" tall, 4½" wide.
Often seen. Designer: Jensen.

Recent price range, $150.00 – 300.00.

Ostrich, #6981.
Year unknown.
Never seen. Designer: Jensen.

First mold July, 1947; estimated auction value, $300.00 – 500.00.

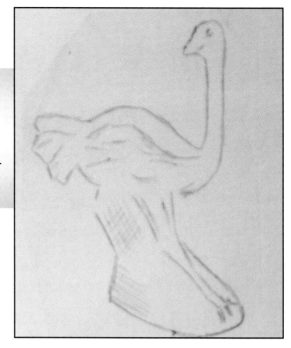

Small Duck, #6992.
1952, 4½" tall, 5½" wide.
Hard to find. Designer: Jensen.

Recent price range, $150.00 – 300.00.

Boxer Dog, Special.
1944, 10½" tall, 10" wide.
Hard to find. Designer: possibly Wareham.

Available in two polychrome styles (one with a lighter tan body and one with a darker chocolate body) and also in bisque white; with base; recent price range, $800.00 – 1,200.00, although a particularly attractive example did sell for over $2,000.00.

MISCELLANEOUS SHAPES

As we pointed out in the previous section, the majority of animal-related shapes designed and sold by Rookwood were functional. Besides paperweights and bookends, this functionality extended to a wide variety of shapes useful in a household of the period from 1900 to 1950. Rookwood obviously saw this as a good means of selling more pottery. We have not attempted to accurately count them, but we estimate there are several hundred trays, flower holders, candleholders, etc., that utilize an animal shape to entice the consumer.

This compilation includes 56 of these numbered miscellaneous shapes and one special miscellaneous shape. We find them a fun and interesting extension of our bookend, paperweight, and animal figural collections.

Guide to Miscellaneous Shapes

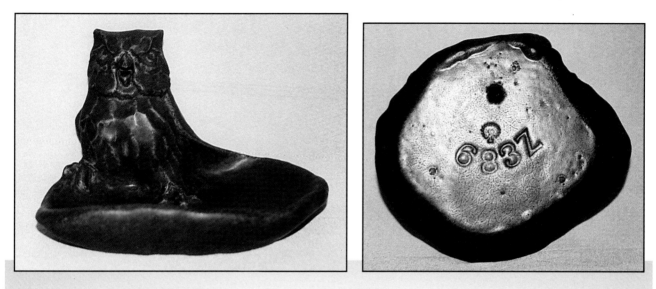

Owl Ashtray, #683Z.
1903, 5" tall, 6½" wide.
Rare. Designer: unknown.

First mold 1903; became Owl paperweight #1084 when introduced into regular shape line; estimated auction value, $400.00 – 700.00.

Elk B.P.O.E. Tray, #744Z.
1904, 1" tall, 5" diameter.
Rare. Designer: unknown.

See special paperweight with similar elk design on page 101; recent price range, $100.00 – 250.00.

Bat Ashtray, #994.
1922, 2½" tall, 6" wide.
Hard to find. Designer: unknown.

Not recognizable as an ashtray from Peck's drawing; recent price range, $200.00 – 400.00.

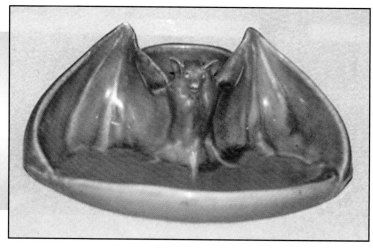

Rook Inkwell, #998.
1922, 7" tall, 10" wide.
Hard to find. Designer: unknown.

Original cost $10.00 for mat, $15.00 polychrome; recent price range, $600.00 – 1,000.00.

Rook Ashtray, #1139.
1946, 4" tall, 7½" wide.
Common. Designer: Wareham.

Original cost $3.50 for mat; among most common of animal shapes; available in both mat and high glaze, and in a wide variety of colors; pooling of glaze in tray (as shown in photo) is a common problem with this shape; recent price range, $100.00 – 200.00.

Miscellaneous Shapes

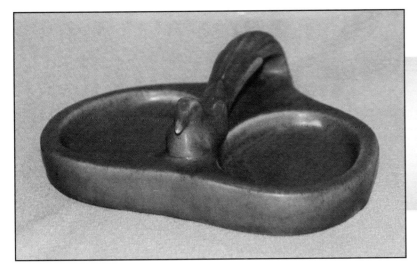

Bird of Paradise Tray, #1210.
1905, 2" tall, 5¾" wide.
Hard to find.
Designer: Shirayamadani.

Original cost $1.50; recent price range, $250.00 – 400.00.

Swan Pin Tray, #1213.
1922, 2" tall, 6" wide.
Common. Designer: unknown.

First mold November 1905; original cost $2.00 mat; recent price range, $150.00 – 300.00.

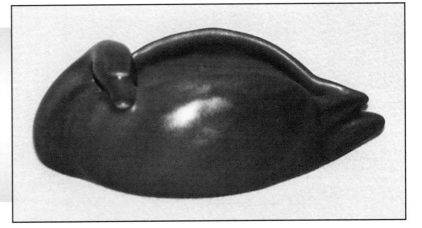

Locust Wall Pocket, #1636.
1920, 8½" tall, 4½" wide, 2½" deep.
Hard to find.
Designer: Shirayamadani.

Original cost $3.50 mat; usually found in mat green, brown, and blue; recent price range, $700.00 – 1,000.00.

Seahorse Candlestick, #1773.
1928, 4" tall, 2½" wide.
Rare. Designer: Toohey.

Original cost $2.00 each for mat; recent price range, $250.00 – 400.00.

Rook Tea Tile, #1794.
1925, 5½" square.
Often seen. Designer: unknown.

Recent price range, $450.00 – 550.00.

Rook and Oak Leaf Inkstand, #2012.
1921, 3" tall, 9½" wide.
Hard to find. Designer: unknown.

First mold November 1911; original cost $5.00 mat; recent price range, $500.00 – 800.00, although one example did sell for over $1,200.00.

Miscellaneous Shapes

Rook and Oak Leaf Pin Tray, #2024.
1914, 3" tall, 11" wide.
Hard to find. Designer: unknown.

Recent price range, $400.00 – 600.00.

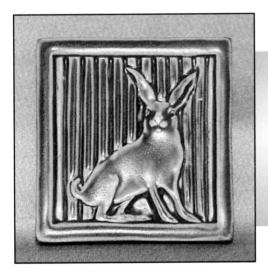

Rabbit Tile, #2052.
1919, 3½" square.
Rare. Designer: unknown.

First mold March 1913; original cost $1.00 mat; very similar to Rabbit paperweight #2056; estimated auction value, $300.00 – 500.00.

Squirrel Tile, #2053.
1921, 3" tall, 5" wide.
Rare. Designer: unknown.

Original cost $1.00 mat; very similar to Squirrel paperweight #2058; estimated auction value, $300.00 – 500.00.

Elephant Tile, #2054.
1921, 3¾" square.
Hard to find. Designer: unknown.

Very similar to Elephant paperweight #2055; original cost $1.00 mat; recent price range, $300.00 – 500.00.

Fish on Clamshell Flower Holder, #2251.
1924, 3½" tall, 5½" wide.
Rare. Designer: unknown.

First mold July 1915; original cost $2.50; estimated auction value, $150.00 – 250.00.

Pan Flower Holder, #2336.
1921, 7" tall, 5" wide.
Often seen. Designer: Haswell.

Original cost $5.00 mat; many examples will have poor mold definition; recent price range, $300.00 – 500.00.

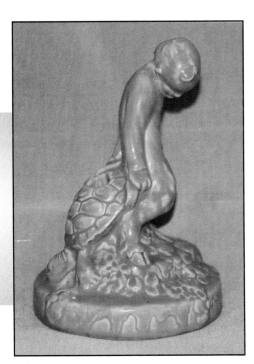

Miscellaneous Shapes 🌟

Frog Doorstop, #2361.
1917, 5" tall, 6½" wide.
Rare. Designer: McDonald.

Original cost $3.50; recent price range, $800.00 – 1,000.00, although a recent sale of over $1,800.00 was recorded.

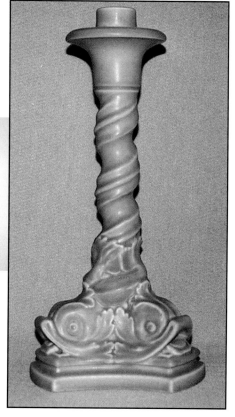

Dolphin Candleholder, #2464.
1921, 11½" tall, 5½" wide.
Hard to find. Designer: McDonald.

Original cost $8.00 for mat; recent price range, $500.00 – 800.00 for a pair.

Sphinx Inkstand, #2504.
1920, 8½" tall, 7½" wide.
Hard to find. Designer: Abel.

First mold December 1919; this example is missing the inkwell insert and cover; estimated auction value, $500.00 – 800.00; with all parts present, $1,000.00 – 1,500.00.

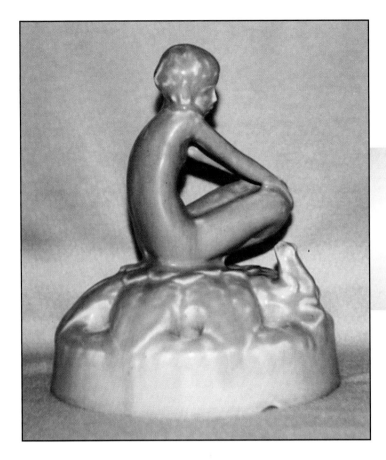

Nude with Frog Flower Holder, #2527.
1922, 6" tall, 5" wide.
Often seen. Designer: Abel.

Recent price range, $200.00 – 300.00.

Three Horses Flower Holder, #2539.
1921, 6" tall, 4½" wide.
Rare. Designer: McDonald.

We have seen only one of these; estimated auction value,
$350.00 – 450.00.

Frog Pin Tray, #2602.
Both 1930; 3¼" tall.
Hard to find. Designer: Shirayamadani.

Recent price range, $600.00 – 1,000.00; however, a single example with a particularly desirable glaze sold for over $2,000.00.

Crocodile Ashtray, #2605.
1943, 2¼" tall, 7" wide.
Rare. Designer: Shirayamadani.

Mold detail on crocodile is usually excellent; recent price range, $500.00 – 800.00.

Cat Doorstop, #2637.
Front and back shown, 1922; 9" tall, 7" wide.
Rare. Designer: unknown.

Note indentation for door on rear of this shape; recent price range, $1,500.00 – 2,000.00.

Fox Ashtray, #2647.
1942, 2¼" tall, 7" wide.
Common. Designer: Shirayamadani.

Among most common of animal shapes; original cost $4.00; recent price range, $150.00 – 250.00.

Miscellaneous Shapes

Seal Ashtray, #2668.
1929, 4" tall, 7" wide.
Hard to find. Designer: Shirayamadani.

Recent price range, $500.00 – 750.00.

Bird Flower Holder, #2710.
1926, 6" tall, 5" wide.
Often seen. Designer: Shirayamadani.

Recent price range, $200.00 – 300.00.

Frog Flower Holder, #2712.
1923, 3½" tall, 4½" wide.
Hard to find. Designer: Shirayamadani.

Recent price range, $250.00 – 350.00.

Frog Ashtray, #2765.
1943, 1¼" tall, 5½" wide.
Often seen. Designer: Shirayamadani.

Original cost $2.50; recent price range,
$200.00 – 300.00.

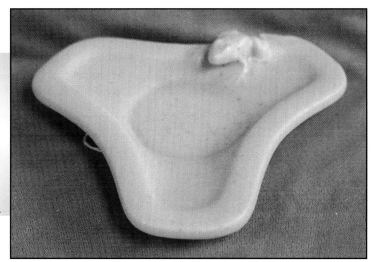

Jay on Tubes Flower Holder, #2798.
1924, 5¼" tall, 5½" wide.
Often seen. Designer: Shirayamadani.

Same jay figure as on bookend #2829; recent price range,
$200.00 – 300.00.

Bat Match Holder, #2939.
1930, 2½" tall, 6" wide.
Hard to find. Designer: Shirayamadani.

Watch out for repaired ears; recent price
range, $250.00 – 350.00.

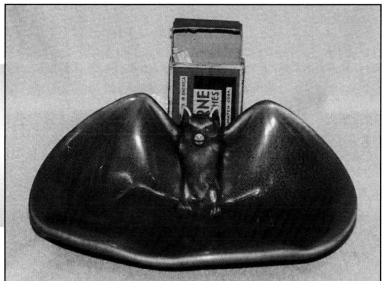

Miscellaneous Shapes

Frog Flower Holder, #2980.
1930, 2½" tall, 3½" wide.
Hard to find. Designer: Shirayamadani.

Recent price range, $300.00 – 500.00.

Turtle Flower Holder, #2994.
1929, 3" tall, 3½" wide.
Hard to find. Designer: Shirayamadani.

Recent price range, $300.00 – 500.00.

Fish Candleholder, #6057.
1928, 4½" tall, 5" wide.
Hard to find. Designer: Shirayamadani.

Recent price range, $200.00 – 400.00.

Fish Letter Holder, #6058.
1930, 7½" tall, 13" wide.
Hard to find.
Designer: Shirayamadani.

Original cost $50.00 for oxblood,
$15.00 – 18.00 for porcelain,
$12.00 for mat; recent price range,
$400.00 – 600.00.

Elephant Candleholder, #6059.
1933, 4" tall, 5" wide.
Often seen. Designer: Shirayamadani.

Recent price range, $200.00 – 400.00.

Fish Candleholder, #6060.
1928, 4" tall, 4" wide.
Hard to find. Designer: Shirayamadani.

Recent price range, $200.00 – 400.00.

Miscellaneous Shapes ☀

Elephant Compote, #6062.
1929, 6" tall, 11" diameter.
Rare. Designer: Shirayamadani.

Estimated auction value, $400.00 – 800.00.

Frog Ash Holder, #6097.
1934, 3" tall, 4" wide.
Often seen. Designer: Shirayamadani.

Original cost $2.50 plain, $3.00 two-tone; recent price range, $200.00 – 350.00.

Pelican Ash Receiver, #6149.
Left, 1937; right, 1934; 4¼" tall, 6" wide.
Often seen. Designer: Shirayamadani.

Original cost $2.50 mat, $3.00 two-tone; recent price range, $200.00 – 300.00.

Puffin Lidded Jar, #6322.
1934, 4" tall, 4" diameter.
Rare. Designer: Shirayamadani.

Recent price range, $250.00 – 400.00.

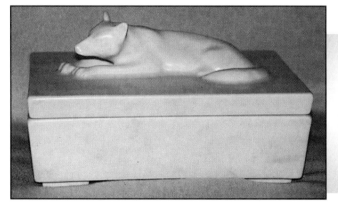

Fox Lidded Box, #6339.
1934, 4¼" tall, 7" wide.
Hard to find. Designer: Wareham.

Fox from #2679, lid from #6205 (see Peck's book for shape number guide); see also Pelican #6340, Fish #6341, and Seal #6342; original cost $10.00; recent price range, $300.00 – 500.00.

Elephant Finial, #6348E.
1935, 1½" tall, 1¾" wide.
Rare. Designer: Conant.

Made for adorning the top of a stack of four concentric circular disks; original cost $5.00 for complete set; undoubtedly the smallest Rookwood animal figural we have seen; estimated auction value, $200.00 – 400.00.

Fish Relish Dish, #6387.
1937, 7" tall, 9½" wide.
Hard to find. Designer: Conant.

Recent price range, $200.00 – 400.00.

Miscellaneous Shapes

Owl Cigarette Holder, #6396.
1932, 4¼" tall, 4" wide.
Rare. Designer: Shirayamadani.

Two compartments, one for matches and one for cigarettes; recent price range, $250.00 – 400.00.

Mandarin Duck Lidded Box, #6413.
1933, 6" tall, 4½" wide.
Hard to find. Designer: Conant.

Original cost $5.00; recent price range, $300.00 – 500.00.

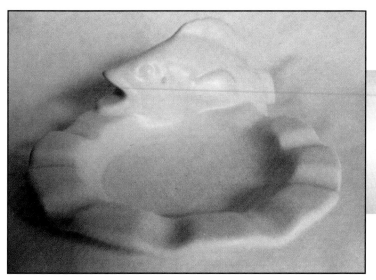

Fish Ashtray, #6500.
1945, 3" tall, 6" diameter.
Hard to find. Designer: Shirayamadani.

Original cost $3.50; recent price range, $200.00 – 400.00.

Fish Ashtray, #6515.
1935, 1¾" tall, 5¼" wide.
Often seen. Designer: Shirayamadani.

Original cost $1.50; recent price range, $150.00 – 300.00.

Penguin Ashtray, #6517.
1935, 4¾" tall, 5½" wide.
Hard to find. Designer: unknown.

Original cost $4.00; Penguin from #2727; recent price range, $400.00 – 600.00.

Donkey Ashtray, #6577.
1936, 4" tall, 5" wide.
Rare. Designer: Shirayamadani.

This donkey shape is not seen elsewhere; recent price range, $300.00 – 500.00.

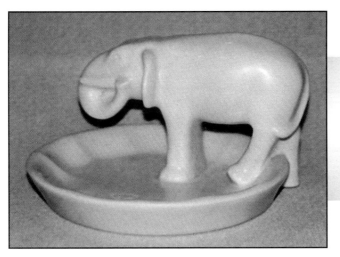

Elephant Ashtray, #6583.
1936, 3" tall, 5½" wide.
Rare. Designer: Shirayamadani.

Three feet in, one foot out! Recent price range, $300.00 – 500.00.

Puffin Ashtray, #6598.
1936, 3" tall, 4½" wide.
Hard to find. Designer: Shirayamadani.

Recent price range, $200.00 – 400.00.

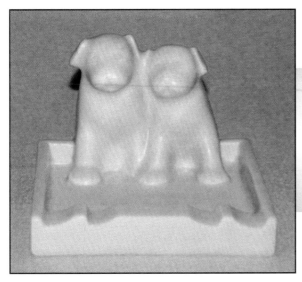

Dog Ashtray, #6624.
1937, 2½" tall, 4" wide.
Hard to find. Designer: Shirayamadani.

This shape is more often referred to by collectors as the "Puppies Ashtray"; recent price range, $400.00 – 700.00.

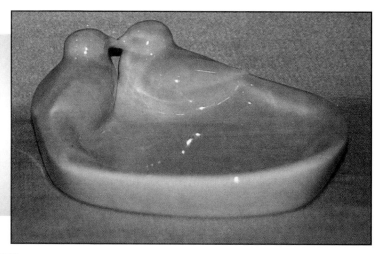

Lovebird Tray, #6990.
1948, 2" tall, 7" wide.
Often seen. Designer: Zanetta.

First mold September 1947; recent price range, $250.00 – 350.00.

Panther Clock Case, #7039.
1951, 7½" tall, 6½" wide, 6" deep.
Hard to find. Case by Wareham, Panther by McDonald.

See Reclining Panther bookend #2564 for panther design; recent price range, $300.00 – 500.00.

Duck Pin Tray, Special.
1929, 2¾" tall, 3½" wide.
Often seen. Designer: unknown.

Base of tray has inscribed "Associated Harvard Clubs, Thirty First Annual Meeting Cincinnati 1929"; recent price range, $200.00 – 400.00.

ROOKWOOD IDENTIFICATION MARKS

It perhaps goes without saying that the integrity of any pottery collection is dependent on the collector's ability to properly identify individual examples of the collection. In this respect, the collector of Rookwood is fortunate – Cincinnati's premier pottery being among the "best-marked" of its time.

On the base of nearly all Rookwood pots, a collector can find the "reverse RP with flames" factory mark, the year of production in Roman numerals (for pots made after the year 1900), and the shape number. Additionally, there may be designer's initials, decorator's signatures, a size symbol, a clay designation, miscellaneous process marks, and a series of "esoteric marks." A complete description of Rookwood's marks appears in the Edwin J. Kircher foreword to The Glover Collection, Cincinnati Art Galleries, 1991, Cincinnati, Ohio.

For the collector of bookends, paperweights and animal figurals (hereafter referred to as BP & AF's) understanding all the complexities of Rookwood identification marks is not necessary. The purpose of this section is to pare these complexities to manageable levels.

Figure 1: Markings on the base of a typical BP & AF.

Figure 1 is a view of a typical base of a BP & AF piece. Essential elements include the following:

Rookwood Factory Mark

The reverse RP factory mark was first introduced by Rookwood in the mid-1880's. Beginning in 1887, one "flame" mark per year was introduced until in 1900 the mark consisted of 14 "flames" surrounding the central RP. This mark was then continued throughout the remaining lifetime of the pottery. Since nearly all BP & AF collectibles were produced after 1900, today's collector needs only to be concerned with the 14-flame mark.

Date of Production

The year of production of a Rookwood pot made prior to 1901 can be discerned by counting the number of flames. Beginning in 1901, Roman numerals were stamped below the reverse RP mark to convey date of production. The flower holder base in Figure 1 shows 1921 (XXI) to be its production year.

The Shape Number

Rookwood kept meticulous records of the shapes produced over the years. These shape records are preserved in the Cincinnati Historical Society Research Library and are available for scholarly study. Herbert Peck, in *The Second Book of Rookwood Pottery*, has done collectors a tremendous service by publishing a compilation of these shapes. Figure 1 shows a shape number of 2336 – which Peck confirms is the Pan Flower Holder.

Shape numbers were assigned consecutively, and therefore bear no direct relationship to the year of production. One can estimate year of *first* production of a given shape number using the chart on the following page. Place the shape number on the line, then drop perpendicularly to the x-axis to find the year the shape was first produced. (Notice that shape numbers 1398 – 1612 and 3000 – 6000 were reserved for Faience Department usage.) This can be useful when examining any Rookwood items that are suspiciously marked. If the marked year of production is *earlier* than found using this chart, it might not be genuine Rookwood.

FIRST YEAR OF PRODUCTION BY SHAPE

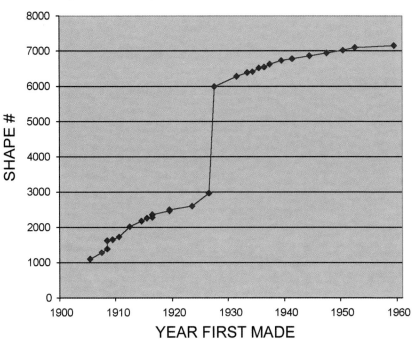

Figure 2: Shape number vs. year of first production.

Occasionally one will find pieces marked with a shape number followed by a Z (see Owl Ashtray #683Z and Elk B.P.O.E. Tray #744Z, for example). This so-called "Z-line" designation indicates the item was made in the 1900 – 1905 time frame when Rookwood was experimenting with mat finishes. There is no simple way to reconcile these Z numbers with the regular line of shape numbers. Some, but not all, of the Z-line shapes are recorded in the shape card catalog preserved in the Cincinnati Historical Society Research Library. For a few items, the Z-line shape was subsequently reproduced in the regular shape line – Owl Ashtray #683Z became Owl paperweight #1084.

Factory Seconds and "Giveaways"

Rookwood items are sometimes found with a wheel-ground "X" cut into the underside of the piece. This indicates the item is of secondary quality owing to some flaw in the making. Sometimes these flaws are readily apparent and significantly reduce value. Other times pieces marked with an X have very minor

flaws, difficult to detect even by seasoned collectors. The X mark should be considered a flag – causing the interested collector to carefully examine before purchasing.

Items with an additional line through the X, producing a mark that resembles a crude star shape, were considered "giveaways." Items marked as giveaways were often taken home by workers, or raffled off to the highest bidder at company sponsored parties for employees. These items generally have severe enough flaws that the collector must think long and hard before deciding to purchase.

Simply recognizing the above few marks will allow casual collectors to identify all that they need to know about BP & AF class members. Below are a few additional marks of which the more advanced collector might wish to be aware.

Size Designation

If applicable, the designation of different sizes of individual shapes was accomplished by placing a letter after the shape number. For example, the Trunk-Down Elephant was made in a larger size, marked with the shape number #2444C, and a smaller size #2444D (see size-comparison photo on page 18.)

Porcelain Symbol

Rookwood introduced a "soft-porcelain" or "semi-porcelain" body in 1915, presumably to allow the use of lighter colors by their decorators. This body was identified with a letter "P" impressed on the base of the item. Quite a number of early bookends were made with this new body. Some of them were polychrome, taking advantage of the better color retention properties; however, most were finished in traditional solid mat. These are still the favorites of many collectors, as evidenced by their elevated auction values (see Bookends section).

Rookwood Identification Marks

Special Shapes

Shapes not in the ordinary sales line were impressed with the letter "S" on the base. Such shapes of BP & AF's are usually commemorative items produced for some special event or, in a few cases, figurals made at the request of a pottery worker. See for example the Hebrew Union College bookends, the Boxer Dog figural, the Harvard Second Triennial paperweight, or the Duck Pin Tray.

Figure 3: Example of a porcelain "P" symbol on the base of a bookend.

Designers' Initials and Decorators' Signatures

BP & AF's were designed by many different Rookwood personnel (see the compilations in the previous sections). Only six of these designers included their initials or names in the molds. William P. McDonald's initials (WPMcD) are found on the backs of many bookends and on the bases of many paperweights, as is Sallie Toohey's "S" overlaid on a "T," and Louise Abel's "A" inside a circle. The initials KB (K. Brown) are found on the Gazelle paperweight #6528 and the Chow Dog bookend #6584. The name J. Reich

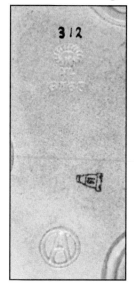

Figure 4: Base of BP & AF identifying Abel as designer.

is found on the Fisherman #6808, and some (but, curiously, not all) examples of the Reader bookend #2184 have Haswell's initials impressed on the back.

Occasionally one will see artist-signed BP & AF's. Usually these were done after 1946 by the artists in Lois Furakawa's "junior decorator" department.

Rooster paperweight #6030, Squirrel paperweight #6025 and Cat paperweight #6065 are sometimes seen decorated and signed. Very few BP & AF's decorated and signed by established Rookwood artists have been seen. However, we know of a Rooster bookend (shape #6386) that was signed under the glaze, "A. Conant." Perhaps this was a presentation piece since this was not Conant's usual signature (his pieces were normally signed with a "C" inside a box), and this bookend also had an unusual glaze. The 1994 Rookwood IV auction conducted by Cincinnati Art Galleries listed two Pheasant (shape #2832) figurals, one signed by Sara Sax and one by William E. Hentschel.

Finishers' Dots

Returning one more time to Figure 1, the remaining mark to be explained is the small dot on the right side of the flames. One sees such dots on many Rookwood pots, especially those produced in the early part of the twentieth century. Until recently, Rookwood researchers and collectors were at a loss to explain their significance.

In 1998, we published an article (*Journal of the American Art Pottery Association*, January – February 1998, Volume 14, Number 1, page 12) solving the mystery of "finishers' dots." (The "finisher" was the person who prepared the individual pot for further treatment. For thrown vases it would have been the thrower. For molded pieces it was the person who removed the pot from the mold and smoothed away the rough edges.) To identify individual finishers Rookwood placed a dot in a prescribed position around the reverse RP factory mark, the date, or the shape number. The dots were placed on the pots in the green stage — at the same time as the other three marks were impressed.

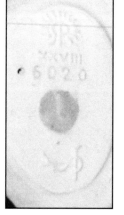

Figure 6: Base of BP & AF identifying Toohey as designer.

Figure 5: Base of BP & AF identifying McDonald as designer.

Rookwood Finishers' Marks, circa 1915 – 1933

Munson
·

Kenkel ·   · Maher

Westerback ·   · Albersman

· Kremer

· Wegesser

Hunt · XXX · Miller

Menzel · 1678 · Dawson

·
Ewan

Figure 7: Template used to place dots identifying individual finishers.

Using the "decoder" shown in Figure 7, one can identify the finisher of a specific pot. This decoder was found among the surviving papers of Harold Bopp, superintendent of Rookwood facilities during the 1930s. Some of the names of finishers are immediately recognizable. Reuben Earl Menzel was employed by Rookwood in various capacities from 1896 to 1959. He was a master potter and headed Rookwood's finishing department for a good portion of his career. Albert Cyrus "Bert" Munson worked in Rookwood's finishing room for 50 years. Ray Dawson worked as a mold-maker and potter prior to moving to Kenton Hills Porcelains in 1939. Jonathan Browne Hunt was a potter for Rookwood for a few years in the 1920s before moving to Newcomb in 1927. Kenkel, Maher, Albersman, Kremer, Wegesser, Miller, Ewan, and Westerback are not mentioned in historical records we have examined.

Figure 8: View of the base of a BP & AF identifying Maher as finisher.

Figure 10: View of the base of a BP & AF identifying Albersman as finisher.

Figure 9: View of the base of a BP & AF identifying Munson as finisher.

Figure 11: View of the base of a BP & AF identifying Ewan as finisher.

CAVEAT EMPTOR

Let the buyer beware! Every collector of art pottery should pay heed to this ancient admonition. The collector of Rookwood bookends, paperweights, and animal figurals must be particularly alert. "New" Rookwood as opposed to "old" Rookwood, repairs and/or restorations, outright fakes, shape reproductions, items marked Rookwood that aren't really Rookwood — all these are out there in the marketplace waiting to ambush the unwary.

"New" As Opposed To "Old" Rookwood

In 1982, Dr. Art Townley, a Michigan dentist and art pottery collector, learned that a group of Florida investors was planning to purchase the remaining assets of The Rookwood Pottery Company from Herschede Hall, the firm that owned Rookwood in 1967, when its doors closed for the last time. These Florida investors apparently planned to ship the surviving Rookwood molds to Korea whereafter mass reproduction would ensue.

Concerned that this would result in flooding of the U.S. market with such reproductions and fearful of the effect this would have on values of authentic Rookwood, Dr. Townley and his wife outbid the Floridians. What they acquired included molds, copyrights, patent rights, shape books, glaze and clay formulas, corporate notes, and medals won by Rookwood over the years.

Although Dr. and Mrs. Townley had no prior experience in pottery making, they were quick learners and in 1983 began producing what they called "Present Day" Rookwood. Production has continued unabated, so much so that to date many thousands of figurals, bookends, and paperweights have been put into circulation.

First examples distributed by the Townleys were

Figure 12: Townley Cat paperweight #6402, made in 1989.

Figure 13: Townley Flying Fish bookend #6482, made in 1995.

marked on the base with the Rookwood "flame," the logo "Present Day Rookwood," and the year of production of the item over the original shape number;

Figure 14: Townley Golden Monkey paper- weight, made in 1983.

Figure 16: Townley Nude Woman book- end #6195.

Figure 15: Townley Ladybug paperweight #6595, made in 1992.

Figure 17: Townley Cocker Spaniel #7024, made in 1988.

for example, 1989/6402 for the Conant Cat paper- weight. Somewhere around 1990 the "Present Day Rookwood" logo was dropped, leaving production since that time marked with just the Rookwood "flame," the year, and the original shape number.

A special production of 2,500 "golden" paper- weights appeared during the mid-1980s. These gold- en colored figurals were originally sold as numbered sets but now are seen regularly as individual offerings to collectors. As an example, the Golden Monkey paperweight is marked on the base with "Golden Monkey, Rookwood Pottery 1983, Original Design by KS, 24 Carat Gold Finish, Limited Edition 2500," and the number "152" in hand script, apparently meaning number 152 out of 2,500.

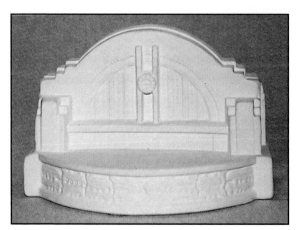

Figure 18: Townley Union Terminal bookend #6376.

Townley figurals are seen in a variety of colors. High glaze is more common than mat — this may simply be collector choice, as both finishes are offered.

Following are the shapes the Townleys have produced as of the middle of 2001:

Paperweights

Turtle	#1686
Pelican	#2711
Duck	#6064
Monkey	#6084
Rabbit	#6160
Cat	#6182
Canary	#6383
Cat	#6402
Hawk	#6405
Goose	#6446
Elephant	#6490
Ladybug	#6595
Duck	#6992
Cocker Spaniel	#7024

Bookends

Large Owl	#2656
Nude Woman	#6159
Union Terminal	#6376
Flying Fish	#6482
Honey Bear	#6485

Just before this manuscript went to the publisher, in the middle of 2001, we began to see examples of a Townley-made advertising tile, 8" x 4", embossed with the outline of a rook on a tree branch. The back of the tile was marked with shape #1622, year 2001, and 66/500 indicating a limited edition. One example was red with gray and white specks, with a semi-gloss glaze. This demonstrates that the Townleys are still in business and will continue to produce additions to their line.

It is important to point out that since the Townleys purchased rights to the Rookwood name and to the use of the Rookwood molds, their offerings should not be considered fakes or illegal reproductions. "New" Rookwood and "old" Rookwood are simply separate classes of collectibles, with the further differentiation that "new" Rookwood is still in production, while "old" Rookwood is not.

In terms of monetary value, they are certainly considered separate classes by collectors. "Old" Rookwood items sell for 10 to 50 times as much as "new" items. Following are a few examples of collector prices:

Townley Turtle #1686 typically sells for $30.00 – 40.00. "Old" Rookwood Turtle #1686 typically sells for $300.00 – 600.00.

Townley Cat #6402 typically sells for $30.00 – 40.00. "Old" Rookwood Cat #6402 sells for $600.00 – 900.00.

Townley Union Terminal bookends #6378 typically sell for $100.00 – 150.00/pair. "Old" Rookwood Union Terminal bookends sell for $5,000.00 – 7,500.00/pair.

It is very important that the Rookwood bookend, paperweight, and animal figural collector learn to differentiate between "old" and "new" Rookwood. We have seen several cases where unaware collectors have purchased "new" Rookwood and paid "old" prices. And we know of one instance where a "new" Cocker Spaniel paperweight #7024 (Figure 17) was found with its base altered to make it appear more like an "old" piece.

Repairs and Restorations

Bookends and paperweights were made to be used. That they were is evident from the amount of damage found on many surviving pieces. Ears were broken, feet were torn from bases, and beaks were chipped. With the rather recent proliferation of pottery repair businesses, we are now finding numerous repaired bookends, paperweights, and animal figurals for sale. Most times such repairs are pointed out by sellers — but not always.

The collector's best weapon when damage is not claimed is a good magnifying glass. The majority of repairs on these pieces were done, not by the well-known and expensive restorers of more valuable vases, but by less experienced, less competent and, therefore, less costly repair services. This helps the wary collector in that repairs are more easily detected. Look for (1) poor color matching, (2) a change in glaze feel around suspect areas, (3) a change in levels of crazing (if crazing exists), and (4) a change in the way light is reflected off repaired surfaces when compared with unrepaired surfaces.

Whenever possible, get a guarantee from the seller that the item has no uncalled damage and no hidden repairs. This will give the collector a chance to inspect more closely, perhaps using a blacklight, and in suspect cases using a little dab of acetone, to determine whether the surface is pristine (never do this without the seller's/owner's consent.)

Outright Fakes

Fortunately there are not many of these. Unfortunately there are some. We have seen two examples. First is a 5" tall, 5" wide three-sided vase with molded owl heads on each of the three faces. This pot is marked on the bottom with the Rookwood "flame," the shape #2972, and the date XXIX (1929). These marks are indistinguishable from authentic Rookwood markings. However, when one goes to the shape records, it is found that #2972 is in reality a 5½" cylindrical vase with no molded images thereon. Further, this three-sided owl vase has also been seen with a Weller factory mark on its base. Finally, these same marks (the flame, #2972, and XXIX) have appeared on other vases that don't match any shapes Rookwood is known to have made. The inescapable conclusion is that someone out

Figure 20: Fake Indian princess bookend sold as Rookwood.

there is producing vases with fake Rookwood (and other) markings.

A second example of this kind of fake is a set of bookends that was recently purchased through an Internet auction site. A female figure, perhaps an Indian maiden, with what appear to be outstretched wings, is depicted. It is a very pleasant shape indeed. These bookends have an authentic-looking set of Rookwood marks on the base — but the shape is not one Rookwood is known to have made.

Close inspection reveals that the Rookwood "flame," the shape #2123, and the year XXIII (1923) have been inserted as a block into the base of each of the bookends. The collector should be on the lookout, for these marks may appear on other shapes!

Shape Reproduction

We have seen only a few examples of copied Rookwood shapes. One, the common Rook Ashtray (#1139), is shown in the photograph on the following page. Found in a Dollar General store, it is unmarked on the base. A second example, reproduced Rook bookends (#2275), was seen in an antique mall in Columbus, Ohio. They also were unmarked and not well made. Slightly smaller than authentic Rooks, this pair was poorly defined with a glaze and color easily

Figure 19: Fake three-sided owl vase sold as Rookwood.

Figure 21: Authentic-looking Rookwood marks on fake bookend, shown in Figure 20.

Figure 22: Reproduction of Rookwood Rook Ashtray.

recognizable as non-Rookwood.

That few reproductions are around is probably due to collectors not being easily fooled. When pottery items appear without typical Rookwood logos — "flame," date, shape number — seasoned collectors simply refuse to buy. This should serve as excellent advice for the beginner.

Items Marked "Rookwood" That Aren't Really Rookwood

Recently we have seen porcelain animal figurals bearing the "REBA Rookwood" mark on their bases. As far as we can determine, although these figurals bear the name Rookwood, they are in no way related to authentic Rookwood pottery.

BIBLIOGRAPHY

Hahn, Frank. "Rookwood Paperweights." *The Antique Trader Weekly*, January 12, 1994.

Kircher, Edwin J. *The Glover Collection*. Cincinnati Art Galleries, 1991, Cincinnati, Ohio.

Nicholson, Nick and Jim Fleming. "Rookwood Paperweights and Animal Figurines." *Journal of the American Art Pottery Association*, July – August 1995, 12 – 20.

Nicholson, Nick and Marilyn Nicholson. "Connecting the Dots." *Journal of the American Art Pottery Association*, January – February 1998, Volume 14, Number 1, 12 – 13.

Peck, Herbert. "The History and Development of Rookwood Bookends." *The Antique Trader,* February 20, 1973, 48.

____. "Rookwood Pottery Paperweights." *Pottery Collectors Newsletter 2*, November 1972, 17.

____. *The Second Book of Rookwood.* Privately printed, 1985, Tucson, Arizona.

Original Rookwood shape numbers are preserved in the Cincinnati Historical Society Research Library and are available during normal business hours.

APPENDIX

Rookwood's main marketing strategy over most of the years it was in business consisted of utilizing franchises — inventory was distributed to selected outlets where it was exposed to the consuming public and eventually sold. Direct sale to consumers was limited, primarily to items sold from the factory showroom or to orders placed for specialized items.

Therefore, advertising directly to consumers was of questionable value. Budget allocations to direct consumer advertising were limited. During the 1910s and 1920s, ads were placed in fashionable magazines of the time, perhaps mostly to be sure customers of franchisers were aware of the Rookwood name.

One other method of direct advertising to the consumer, used sparingly by Rookwood, involved distributing small, inexpensive brochures containing photos of certain sales inventories, along with price lists for these items. In the following pages we reproduce these items:

A bookends brochure and corresponding price list from the early 1920s;

Bookend and novelties brochures, along with corresponding price lists, from the early 1930s.

1920s

2444C Large   2444D Small

ROOKWOOD
BOOK-ENDS

❋

THE ROOKWOOD POTTERY COMPANY
CINCINNATI

2184   2185

THESE book-ends, designed by Rookwood artists, are made in a variety of designs and glazes, with agreeable textures and in colors which make them a pleasant and useful ornament on table or shelf. They have sufficient weight to hold the books firmly upright.

2445   2446

2186   2362

THE prevailing colors are ivory, medium blue, dark blue, olive green, golden brown, yellow, buff and pink. New designs are constantly appearing and other colors are made specially from time to time.

2275   2274

ROOKWOOD products may be secured thru the dealer in your locality, or, in case there should be no dealer, from the Pottery direct. Folders illustrating various other ideas may be had and a separate sheet will show prices and sizes of all articles illustrated in these folders.

❋

The Rookwood Pottery Company
Cincinnati

2447

PRICE LIST *of*

Rookwood Pieces

as illustrated in various folders

WE give herewith the prices of certain undecorated types of plain Mat Glazes and Porcelains which are (the only) designs repeated with some similarity.

The prices are the same at the Pottery or in the hands of our Agents.

If you do not find at our agents what you wish, then select any pieces illustrated in these folders by number and state the price. Remit for the piece or pieces ordered and we will express them to our local agent or direct to you, you to pay expressage on arrival.

Every care will be taken to fill orders exactly as given.

Prices subject to change without notice.

ROOKWOOD BOOK ENDS

Shape No.	Size, Approximately		Price per Pair Mat Glaze Plain Color
	Base, Inches	Height, In.	
2184......	5½ x 6½	6½	$20.00
2185......	3 x 5	5½	7.00
2186......	4½ x 5½	5	12.00
2274......	6 x 6½	6	20.00
2275......	3½ x 5½	5½	7.00
2362......	4½ x 5	7½	10.00
2444C....	4½ x 6½	6	15.00
2444D....	3½ x 5½	4½	10.00
2445......	4 x 5½	4½	7.00
2446......	4 x 4½	5½	7.00
2447......	4 x 5½	5½	5.00

ROOKWOOD CANDLESTICKS

Shape No.	Size, Approximately		Price Per Piece	
	Diameter of Base, In.	Height Inches	Mat Glaze Plain Color	Porcelain
508....	4½	6	.....	$3.50
822C...	5½	8	$4.00	5.00
822D...	4½	6½	3.00	3.50
1067....	4	1½	2.00	2.50
1192....	4½	6½	3.50	4.00
1194....	3½	6½	3.50	4.00
1355....	4½	7	3.50	4.00
1630....	4	9½	5.00	6.00
1635....	3½	7	3.50	4.00
1637....	5	9½	5.00	6.00
1638....	4½	3½	3.00	....
1647....	4½	4½	3.50	....
1773....	3	4	2.00	2.50
2025....	3½	8	4.00	5.00
2198....	6	8	4.00	5.00
2199....	4	6	3.00	3.50
2226....	5	7½	5.00	6.00
2270....	4½	10	....	12.00
2289....	5½	8	7.00	8.00
2304....	5	11	7.00	8.00
2311....	3½	1½	1.50	2.00
2464....	5½	11	8.00	10.00
2473....	4½	2	2.00	2.50

ROOKWOOD BOWLS

Shape No.	Size, Approximately		Mat Glaze Plain Color	Porcelain	
	Height Inches	Diam. Inches		Plain	Two Colors
928C....	5½	11	$12.00	....	....
928D....	5	10	10.00	....	....
928E....	4½	8½	7.00	$8.00	$10.00
957B....	3½	8¾	6.00	8.00	10.00
957D....	3½	7	4.00	5.00	6.00
957DD..	2½	5½	3.00	3.50	4.00
1069......	3	5½	2.50	3.00	3.50
1188......	2	4½	1.50	....	....
1231......	7½	9½	12.00	12.00	15.00
1308......	2½	6	3.00	....	....
1793......	3	6	3.00	4.00	....
1800......	3	5½	2.50	4.00	5.00
1802......	3	5½	2.50	3.50	5.00
1811......	5¾	7	5.00	6.00	7.00
1900......	3½	4½	2.50	3.50	....
1911......	3	5½	2.50	3.00	3.50
2080......	3	5½	2.50	....	....
2106B....	3	11¼	8.00	10.00	12.00
2106C....	3	10	7.00	8.00	10.00
2131......	2½	5	2.00	....	....
2134......	2	6	3.00	3.50	....
2145......	3½	8	5.00	7.00	....
2148......	3	8	5.00	6.00	7.00
2162......	3	8	5.00	....	....
2163B....	3¾	9	6.00	8.00	10.00
2163E....	2	4½	1.50	2.00	2.50
2165......	3½	8¾	6.00	8.00	10.00
2178B....	3	9	6.00	7.00	8.00
2178C....	2½	7½	6.00	7.00	8.00
2178D....	2	6	3.50	3.50	4.00
2179......	4	6	3.50	4.00	5.00
2212......	4½	5½	4.00	4.00	5.00
2222......	5½	5½	5.00	6.00	7.00
2234......	3	4¼	2.00	2.50	3.00
2235......	3¼	6	4.00	5.00	6.00
2244......	4¾	9½	....	....	15.00
2250......	3	14¼	15.00	18.00	20.00
2253C....	3	7½	....	6.00	7.00
2253D....	2½	6½	....	3.50	4.00
2253E....	2	5½	....	2.50	3.00
2256B....	4	10	7.00	8.00	10.00
2256C....	3½	8¼	5.00	6.00	7.00

ROOKWOOD BOWLS — Continued

Shape No.	Size, Approximately		Mat Glaze Plain Color	Porcelain	
	Height Inches	Diam. Inches		Plain	Two Colors
2256D....	2½	6½	3.50	3.50	4.00
2257E....	4¼	5½	....	4.00	5.00
2259C....	5¼	8½	....	8.00	10.00
2259D....	5	7	....	7.00	8.00
2259E....	3½	5½	....	4.00	5.00
2260C....	6¼	9½	....	12.00	15.00
2260D....	5¼	8	7.00	8.00	10.00
2260E....	4½	6½	4.00	5.00	6.00
2261.....	2	5¾	....	2.50	3.00
2262C....	3	10	....	12.00	15.00
2262D....	2¼	7½	5.00	6.00	7.00
2268A....	3½	16	20.00	25.00	30.00
2268B....	3	13	....	18.00	20.00
2287......	3½	8½	....	6.00	7.00
2294A....	5½	17½	25.00	30.00	35.00
2294B....	5	15½	15.00	20.00	25.00
2294C....	4½	13	....	15.00	18.00
2296B....	5½	15	20.00	25.00	30.00
2296C....	5	13¼	18.00	20.00	25.00
2297C....	5½	8½	....	12.00	15.00
2338......	6	6	10.00	10.00	....
2341......	6	7	8.00	10.00	12.00
2346......	4¼	7½	10.00	10.00	10.00

ROOKWOOD VASE FORMS AND LAMP BASES

Shape No.	Size Approx. Height Inches	Mat Glaze Plain Color	Porcelain	
			Plain	Two Colors
92B...	9	$7.00	$8.00	$10.00
339B...	15	20.00	30.00	35.00
497....	8	4.00	....	....
1812....	7½	2.50	....	....
1814....	7	2.50	....	....
1815....	6½	2.00	....	....
1821....	6¼	2.00	2.50	3.00
1822....	6¼	2.50	....	....
1823....	7	3.00	3.50	4.00
1889....	6½	2.50	3.00	3.50
1894....	6½	3.50	....	....
1902....	5¼	2.00	....	....
2088....	5¼	1.50	....	....

ROOKWOOD VASE FORMS and LAMP BASES — Continued

Shape No.	Size Approx. Height Inches	Mat Glaze Plain Color	Porcelain	
			Plain	Two Colors
2089....	4	$1.50	....	....
2093....	3¼	1.50	....	....
2095....	5¼	2.00	....	....
2097....	3¼	1.50	....	....
2109....	5¼	1.50	$2.00	$2.50
2112....	6	1.50	....	....
2114....	6¾	2.00	2.50	3.00
2115....	6¾	2.00	....	....
2121....	7	2.50	....	....
2122....	4½	1.50	....	....
2123....	5½	1.50	2.50	3.00
2124....	5½	2.00	....	....
2125....	5¾	1.50	....	....
2129....	8¾	5.00	6.00	7.00
2135....	5¾	1.50	2.00	2.50
2143....	7¾	3.50	....	....
2172....	10½	5.00	6.00	7.00
2176....	9	5.00	....	....
2298C...	8½	18.00	20.00	25.00
2301E...	8½	6.00	7.00	8.00
2303....	11¼	8.00	10.00	12.00
2316....	8¼	4.00	....	....
2323....	7¾	4.00	....	....
2324....	8	4.00	....	....
2325....	9	7.00	8.00	10.00
2331....	7¾	4.00	....	....
2335....	11½	10.00	12.00	15.00
2371....	17	....	40.00	45.00
2387....	8½	5.00	....	....
2388....	9¼	5.00	....	....
2391....	11	8.00	....	....
2392....	9	5.00	6.00	7.00
2398....	9¾	7.00	....	....
2401....	7¼	3.50	....	....
2405....	9½	7.00	....	....
2408....	14	10.00	....	....
2422....	10¾	8.00	....	....
2438....	7	2.50	....	....
2439....	7¼	3.00	....	....
2442....	16½	....	20.00	25.00
2476....	8¼	5.00	....	....
2478....	7½	3.00	....	....
2482....	11¾	10.00	....	....

ROOKWOOD VASE FORMS and LAMP BASES — Continued

Shape No.	Size Approx. Height Inches	Mat Glaze Plain Color	Porcelain	
			Plain	Two Colors
2483....	10¼	$7.00	....	....
2484....	9½	8.00	....	....
2485....	10	7.00	....	....
2486....	9¾	7.00	....	....
2489....	11¾	10.00	$12.00	$15.00

The following forms are suitable for LAMP BASES, in which case we supply them pierced ready for mounting.

Shape No.	Size Approximately Height, Inches	Mat Glaze Plain Color
614D..............	11	$8.00
837................	10½	12.00
938C..............	8¾	10.00
999C..............	9¼	10.00
1134..............	14	12.00
1282..............	11½	10.00
1283..............	10¾	10.00
1284..............	10¾	10.00
1371..............	15	12.00
1372..............	15	12.00
1664D............	11	8.00
1709..............	10¼	8.00
1712..............	9½	8.00
2032C............	12	10.00
2220..............	8½	8.00
2301B............	12½	18.00
2414..............	9½	8.00
2421..............	9¾	8.00
2491..............	14¾	20.00
2492..............	12¾	12.00

1930s

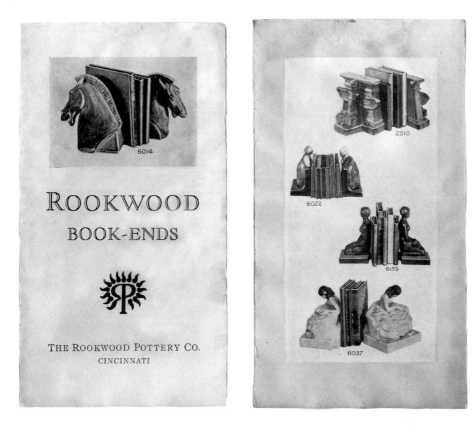

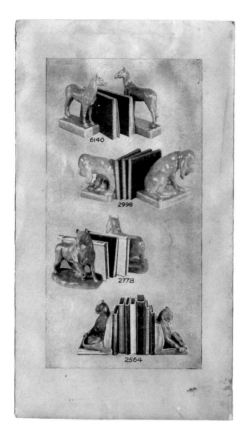

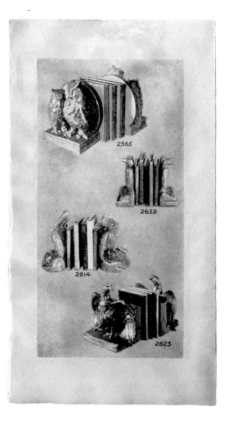

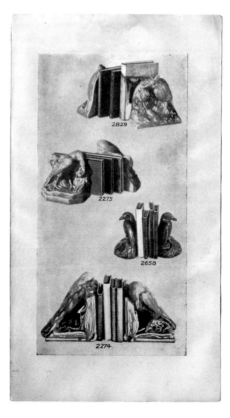

ROOKWOOD BOOK-ENDS

THESE illustrations, in relative size, show some of the many book-ends designed by Rookwood artists. In shape, glaze texture and color they form a pleasing and useful ornament on table or shelf. Their weight is sufficient to hold the books firmly and upright. The prevailing colors are ivory, medium and dark blue, olive green, golden brown, yellow, buff and pink, but other colors are also available and, in some cases, decoration is applied in several colors where that helps to pick out the design. New shapes are constantly appearing and special colors are available.

The work of the Rookwood studios may be secured through the dealer in your locality or, in case there should be no dealer, from the Pottery direct. Folders illustrating various other ideas may be had with prices and sizes.

THE ROOKWOOD POTTERY CO.
CINCINNATI

Appendix

PRICE LIST *of*
Rookwood Pieces
as illustrated in relative sizes on our various folders

WE give herewith the prices of certain undecorated types of plain Mat Glazes and Porcelains which are (the only) designs repeated with some similarity.

The prices are the same at the Pottery or in the hands of our Agents.

If you do not find at our agents what you wish, then select any pieces illustrated in these folders by number and state the price. Remit for the piece or pieces ordered and we will express them to our local agent or direct to you, you to pay expressage on arrival.

Every care will be taken to fill orders exactly as given.

Prices subject to change without notice.

ROOKWOOD VASES

Shape No.	Size Approx. Height Inches	Mat Glaze Plain Color	Porcelain, Hi-Gloss	
			Plain	Two Colors
778	10	....	$6.00	$7.00
902D	8	....	5.00	...
1710	10½	$10.00	....	....
1711	10	8.00	....	....
2072	6	2.50	....	....
2111	6	1.50	....	....
2112	6	1.50	....	....
2246A	19	....	50.00	60.00
2246C	14½	....	25.00	30.00
2272	12	....	15.00	18.00
2282	5½	1.50	....	....
2302	8	....	10.00	12.00
2367	16	....	20.00	....
2372	17	35.00	40.00	45.00
2413	8	5.00	....	....
2426	8	5.00	....	....
2484	9½	8.00	....	....
2511	6½	8.00	10.00	12.00
2528	8½	....	5.00	6.00
2551	14	....	20.00	25.00
2559	4	2.00	....	....
2639E	8	....	5.00	6.00
2640C	14	....	35.00	40.00
2640E	6	10.00	12.00	15.00
2734	8	....	8.00	10.00
2746	9½	....	12.00	15.00
2758	9½	5.00	....	....
2782	9½	7.00	....	....
2783	10	....	10.00	12.00
2784	10	12.00	15.00	18.00
2786	11½	10.00	....	....
2794	9½	5.00	....	....
2812	5	3.50	....	....
2821B	15	....	....	12.00
2827A	17	15.00	18.00	20.00
2838	5	3.50	....	....
2841	5	....	2.50	3.00
2842	5	....	2.50	3.00
2884	6	1.50	....	....
2911	8½	7.00	....	....
2930	10½	12.00	12.00	15.00
2932	14	....	15.00	18.00

ROOKWOOD VASES — Continued

Shape No.	Size Approx. Height Inches	Mat Glaze Plain Color	Porcelain, Hi-Gloss	
			Plain	Two Colors
2933	12	$10.00	$12.00	$15.00
2935	8	....	7.00	8.00
2942	5½	4.00	5.00	6.00
2949	10	....	15.00	18.00
2959	6	2.00	2.50	....
2970	13	....	12.00	15.00
2972	5½	1.50	....	....
2973	8	....	6.00	7.00
2977	7½	5.00	6.00	7.00
2995	19½	35.00	45.00	50.00
2997	14	10.00	....	....
6002	7	....	6.00	7.00
6004	13½	12.00	15.00	18.00
6005C	13	....	12.00	15.00
6005F	7	3.50	4.00	5.00
6006	12	10.00	12.00	15.00
6008C	15	....	18.00	20.00
6008E	10	5.00	6.00	7.00
6015	12½	10.00	12.00	15.00
6028	7½	3.00	....	....
6029	6½	5.00	....	....
6036	6	5.00	6.00	7.00
6043	7	5.00	6.00	7.00
6047	6	3.50	....	....
6050	12	....	15.00	18.00
6053	8	4.00	5.00	6.00
6088	11	10.00	12.00	15.00
6093	4	2.00	....	....
6094	4½	1.50	....	....
6098	4½	2.00	2.50	3.00
6100	5	1.50	....	....
6103	3½	1.50	....	....
6107	4	1.50	....	....
6110	8½	....	8.00	10.00
6111	9	....	10.00	12.00
6115	10	....	12.00	15.00
6119	10	7.00	7.00	8.00
6120	11	8.00	10.00	12.00
6121	7¼	3.50	4.00	....
6147	7	4.00	5.00	6.00
6150	5½	3.50	....	....
6157	5½	3.50	4.00	5.00

ROOKWOOD VASES — Continued

Shape No.	Size Approx. Height Inches	Mat Glaze Plain Color	Porcelain, Hi-Gloss	
			Plain	Two Colors
6162	5	$6.00	$8.00	$10.00
6171	16	....	20.00	....
6175	7	5.00	5.00	....
6179	5	4.00	4.00	....
6181C	8½	....	8.00	10.00
6183F	4½	2.00	2.00	2.50
6184E	7	4.00	4.00	....
6184G	5	....	2.50	3.00
6185D	8½	8.00	8.00	10.00
6185F	5½	2.50	2.50	3.00
6193C	8	7.00	7.00	8.00
6194D	6½	4.00	4.00	5.00
6194F	5	2.50	2.50	3.00
6195C	10	....	7.00	8.00
6195F	6	....	2.00	2.50
6196E	6	3.50	3.50	4.00
6198D	7¼	5.00	5.00	6.00
6199D	5	3.50	3.50	4.00
6200C	9	....	8.00	10.00
6201D	6½	....	4.00	5.00
6203C	8	....	8.00	10.00
6204B	9	....	10.00	12.00
6206D	7½	5.00	5.00	6.00
6211	10	....	8.00	10.00

ROOKWOOD BOWLS

Shape No.	Size, Approx.		Mat Glaze Plain	Porcelain, Hi-Gloss	
	Height Inches	Diam. Inches		Plain	Two Colors
957XX	5½	13	....	$20.00	$25.00
957A	4½	11	....	12.00	15.00
957B	4	9	$6.00	....	....
957C	3	8	5.00	....	....
1351	3	6	3.50	....	....
2098	2	4½	1.50	....	....
2130	2	4½	1.50	....	....
2145	3	8	5.00	....	....
2146	3	8	5.00	....	....
2149	3½	6	6.00	....	....
2160	2½	7	4.00	....	....

ROOKWOOD BOWLS — Continued

Shape No.	Size, Approx.		Mat Glaze Plain	Porcelain, Hi-Gloss	
	Height Inches	Diam. Inches		Plain	Two Colors
6072	2	4¼	$1.50	$2.00	$2.50
6076	3½	4½	2.00	....	....
6086	2½	5	3.00	4.00	5.00
6089	2	3½x5	1.50	2.00	2.50
6113	4	4½	2.00	....	....
6122	3¼	4x6	3.50	3.50	4.00
6129	8	7	10.00	12.00	15.00
6130	3½	7½	8.00	8.00	10.00
6131	5	9	12.00	12.00	15.00
6132	3	7	6.00	6.00	7.00
6135	4½	8½	5.00	6.00	7.00
6165	9	6½x10½	8.00	10.00	12.00

ROOKWOOD FLOWER HOLDERS

Shape No	Height Inches	Diam. Inches	Mat Glaze	Porcelain Hi-Gloss
2281	6½	6	$7.00	$7.00
2338	6	6	10.00	10.00
2527	5¼	4¾	7.00	7.00
2536	5¼	4¾	3.50	3.50
2538	5½	4¾	5.00	5.00
2539	5½	4½	3.50	3.50
2540	5½	4¼	3.50	3.50
2541	5½	4½	3.50	3.50
2542	4¼	4½	3.50	3.50
2702	6	4½	5.00	5.00
2710	5½	4½	5.00	5.00
2712	4	4½	3.50	3.50
2798	5	4¼	5.00	5.00
2801	7	4½	7.00	7.00
2835	3¾	4	3.50	3.50
2850	4½	6¼	15.00	15.00
2851	9	7	25.00	25.00
2979	2½	4	3.50	3.50
2980	2¼	4	2.00	2.00
2994	2¾	3¼	2.00	2.00
6012	3½	4½	4.00	4.00
6087	6	4¼	5.00	5.00

ROOKWOOD BOWLS — Continued

Shape No.	Size, Approx.		Mat Glaze Plain	Porcelain, Hi-Gloss	
	Height Inches	Diam. Inches		Plain	Two Colors
2163B	3¾	9	$6.00	....	....
2163E	2	4½	1.50	....	....
2177	3	8	5.00	....	....
2212	4½	5½	....	$3.50	$4.00
2235	3½	5½	....	5.00	6.00
2258X	2½	13	....	18.00	20.00
2260C	6½	10	....	12.00	15.00
2260D	5¼	8	....	8.00	10.00
2260E	4½	6½	....	5.00	6.00
2294A	5½	17½	....	30.00	35.00
2294B	5	14	....	20.00	25.00
2294C	4	12	....	15.00	18.00
2512	10½	15	75.00	75.00	....
2530	3	11½	8.00	....	....
2532	3	7	4.00	....	....
2574C	3½	13	....	15.00	18.00
2574D	2¾	10½	....	10.00	12.00
2577	3½	6	....	4.00	5.00
2683	3	8	5.00	....	....
2684	5¼	7	....	10.00	12.00
2737	5	6	4.00	6.00	7.00
2741	3¾	5½	3.50	....	....
2760	3¼	7½	....	6.00	7.00
2847	4½	6x10	6.00	6.00	7.00
2848	3	6½x13	....	6.00	7.00
2875	2½	10	....	10.00	12.00
2916	3	6½x12	6.00	6.00	7.00
2922	4½	7x9	....	8.00	10.00
2923	7½	6½x13	15.00	18.00	20.00
2925	2½	11½	....	12.00	15.00
2951	5	10	....	10.00	12.00
2968	5	8½	....	12.00	15.00
2993	5	6½	....	6.00	7.00
6010C	11½	10½	....	25.00	30.00
6010E	8	7	10.00	10.00	12.00
6013	6½	7½	....	8.00	10.00
6033	3½	10	10.00	12.00	15.00
6038	2½	8x11	....	10.00	12.00
6039	3½	11	....	12.00	15.00
6046	6½	6x7½	....	10.00	12.00
6052	5½	6¼	5.00	6.00	7.00
6058	7	4x12	12.00	15.00	18.00
6062	5½	11	18.00	20.00	25.00

ROOKWOOD NOVELTIES

Shape No.	Approx. Height Inches	Approx. Diam. Inches	Mat Glaze Plain Color	Porcelain, Hi-Gloss	
				Plain Color	Two Colors
1084......	4	5½x6½	$4.00	....	....
1321E....	4	....	2.50	....	....
1391......	6	....	4.00	....	....
1669......	....	5 sq.	2.50	....	....
1794......	....	6 sq.	3.50	....	....
1897......	5½	....	5.00	....	....
2008......	7½	....	2.00	....	....
2017......	2½	4½	3.50	....	....
2026......	8	....	10.00	....	....
2456......	4 long	....	3.50	$4.00	$5.00
2578......	....	9½ extreme	....	8.00	10.00
2602......	3½	6½x7	4.00	5.00	....
2605......	....	6x7	4.00	....	....
2641B....	....	5¼	3.00	....	....
2647......	....	6½	4.00	....	....
2655......	5½	....	3.00	....	....
2660D....	....	4½	3.50	....	....
2677......	3½	2½x4	2.00	2.50	....
2679......	....	5½ extreme	2.00	....	....
2727......	5	....	2.50	....	....
2750......	7½	....	3.50	....	....
2756......	....	5 extreme	2.50	....	....
2766......	....	8½	....	7.00	8.00
2777......	5	....	2.50	....	....
2792......	3½	....	2.00	....	....
2797......	3½	....	2.00	....	....
2868......	4¼	....	2.50	....	....
2890......	....	5½	2.00	....	....
2929......	3¼	5½x9½	....	18.00	....
2939......	....	6 extreme	3.50	....	....
2940......	7½	....	1.50	....	....
2952......	3½	....	1.50	....	....
2957......	6¼	....	2.00	....	....
2978......	3	6x7	8.00	10.00	....
3203......	....	6 square	3.50	....	....
6003......	....	4x6	1.50	....	....
6009......	3½	....	1.50	....	....

ROOKWOOD NOVELTIES — Continued

Shape No.	Approx. Height Inches	Approx. Diam. Inches	Mat Glaze Plain Color	Porcelain, Hi-Gloss	
				Plain Color	Two Colors
6025......	4	....	$2.50	....	....
6026......	4	4½ square	3.50	$4.00	$5.00
6030......	5	....	2.50	2.50	....
6064......	2	3¾	1.50	....	....
6065......	2½	....	2.00	....	....
6068......	....	6¼ square	3.00	....	....
6071......	3	....	2.00	....	....
6084......	4	....	2.00	2.50	....
6097......	3	....	2.00	2.50	3.00
6116......	....	6 long	2.50	....	....
6136......	4½	....	8.00	....	....
6151......	....	5½	1.50	....	....
6160......	3¼	....	1.50	2.00	....
6164......	12	5½x9	25.00	25.00	....
6169......	4	....	1.50	....	....
6170......	6¼	....	2.50	3.00	....
6172......	3¼	5½	2.00	2.00	....
6177......	10	11 extreme	25.00	25.00	....
6182......	6½	....	4.00	4.00	....

ROOKWOOD BOOK ENDS

Shape No	Height Inches	PRICE PER PAIR			
		Mat Glaze		Porcelain, Hi-Gloss	
		Plain	Decor-ated	P'ain	Decor-ated
2274......	6½	$20.00	$30.00	....	$30.00
2275......	5	7.00	....	....	....
2444C....	6	15.00	....	....	....
2444D....	5	10.00	....	$10.00	....
2503......	7	10.00	....	....	....
2510......	5½	15.00	....	....	20.00
2564......	5½	12.00	....	15.00	....
2565......	7	15.00	....	....	....
2614......	7	10.00	....	....	....
2623......	6½	15.00	....	....	....
2658......	5½	7.00	....	....	....
2659......	5¾	7.00	....	....	....
2678......	4½	8.00	....	8.00	....
2695......	5½	7.00	....	....	....
2778......	5	10.00	....	....	....
2829......	5½	7.00	....	....	....
2836......	4	7.00	10.00	....	....
2837......	6	7.00	12.00	....	12.00
2998......	5	10.00	....	10.00	....
6014......	6	10.00	....	....	....
6019......	6½	7.00	....	7.00	....
6022......	6	....	12.00	....	....
6037......	6½	7.00	12.00	....	....
6124......	7½	10.00	....	....	....
6140......	6½	10.00	....	10.00	....
6159......	7	10.00	....	10.00	....

ROOKWOOD CANDLESTICKS

Shape No.	Size, Approx.		PRICE—*Pair †Each		
	Height Inches	Base Inches	Mat Glaze Plain	Porcelain, Hi-Gloss	
				Plain	Two Colors
882D....	6½	4½	$5.00*	....	....
1067......	1½	5½	2.00†	....	....
1637......	9½	4¾	4.00†	....	....
1638......	3½	5½	2.50†	....	....
1647......	4½	5½	3.50†	....	....
1773......	4	3	4.00*	....	....
2311......	1½	3½	3.00*	....	....
2497......	13	5	10.00†	$10.00	....
2633......	2	4	3.00*	....	....
2666......	7¾	4	6.00*	....	....
2920......	3	6	3.50†	....	....
2961......	3½	4½	5.00*	6.00	$7.00
2981......	2½	4	4.00*	5.00	....
2992......	3½	4	5.00*	....	7.00
6017......	5	3	4.00*	5.00	6.00
6056......	4½	3	5.00*	6.00	7.00
6057......	4½	5	5.00*	6.00	7.00
6059......	4	3½	5.00*	6.00	7.00
6060......	3½	3½	5.00*	6.00	....
6069......	3	4	5.00*	6.00	....
6118......	5½	3¾	5.00*	7.00	....

INDEX

Index ☀

ABOUT THE AUTHORS

Nick and Marilyn Nicholson, art pottery collectors for the past 15 years, reside in a suburb of Cincinnati, Ohio. Although their collecting focuses on Rookwood (probably because of its abundance in the local area,) their tastes are eclectic — the Nicholsons' collection includes many pieces of Rookwood along with examples of several other pottery makers. In 1998 they published *Kenton Hills Porcelains, Inc.: The Story of a Small Art Pottery 1939 – 1944*, after realizing that little was known concerning their second favorite collectible.

Nick (an Iowa native) and Marilyn (a Nebraskan raised in South Dakota) met in undergraduate school. They are both retired — Nick from more than 29 years as a research manager at Procter & Gamble, and Marilyn from her duties as homemaker (they have two grown children and a new granddaughter) and income tax consultant. They travel extensively and enjoy spending winters at their vacation home on the Gulf Coast. Other vices include golf, and for Nick, fishing.

Nick and Marilyn Nicholson

About the Authors

Jim Thomas grew up collecting antique furniture, American type coins, and Brilliant Period cut glass. It has been only in the last ten years that he has turned his attention to Rookwood pottery and even more recently to bookends and figurals. He taught for 37 years in West Virginia and Ohio schools on the secondary level, serving as English department head at both Dupont High School in Charleston, West Virginia, and at Sycamore High School in a Cincinnati suburb. He retired in 1990, only to move to New Mexico where for three years he wrote policies and procedures for the Las Vegas Medical Center. He has since returned to Cincinnati where he now lives — and collects.

Jim Thomas